HIBISCUS

on the Lake

HIBISCUS
on the Lake

Twentieth-Century Telugu Poetry from India

EDITED AND TRANSLATED BY

VELCHERU NARAYANA RAO

THE UNIVERSITY OF WISCONSIN PRESS

The University of Wisconsin Press
1930 Monroe Street
Madison, Wisconsin 53711

www.wisc.edu/wisconsinpress/

3 Henrietta Street
London WC2E 8LU, England

5   4   3   2   1

Printed in the United States of America

Library of Congress Cataloging-in-Publication Data
Hibiscus on the lake : Twentieth-century Telugu poetry from India
  edited and translated by Velcheru Narayana Rao.
  pp.   cm.
  Includes bibliographical references and index.
  ISBN 0-299-17700-9 (Cloth : alk. paper)
  ISBN 0-299-17704-1 (Paper : alk. paper)
    1. Telegu poetry—Translations into English. 2. Poets, Telugu—Biography.
  I. Narayana Rao, Velcheru, 1932–
  PL4780.65.E5 H53   2002
  894'.8271008—dc21   2001005496

We acknowledge with thanks permission kindly given to translate the work of the
following poets (names of the copyright holders are given in italics after the
names of the poets): Abburi Ramakrishna Rao, *Abburi Chayadevi;*Adivi Bapiraju,
K. Bapiraju; Ajanta, *P. Jayakrishna;* Arudra, *Ramalakshmi Arudra;* Bairagi, *A. Jayakumar;*
Chavali Bangaramma, *Ch. N. V. Prasad;* Chellapilla Venkata Sastri, *C. Venkata Sastry;*
Devarakonda Balagangadhara Tilak, *D.S.Murty;* Devulapalli Krishna Sastri, *D. S.
Sastry (Bujjai);* Duvvuri Ramireddy, *A Venkureddy and Duvvuri Ramireddy Vijnana
Samiti;* Jashuva, *Hemalata Lavanam;* Kavikondala Venkatarao, *K. V. Suryanarayana;*
Nanduri Subbarao, *N.S. Ramarao;* Rayaprolu Subbarao, *Rayaprolu Rajeswari;* Revati
Devi, *Raghuram Reddy;* Sishtla Uma-maheswara Rao, *Sihstla Ramalakshmamma;*
Sri Sri, *Venkata Ramana Srirangam;* Srirangam Narayana Babu, *Ramalakshmi Arudra;*
Tenneti Suri, *Tenneti Chalapathi;* Tripuraneni Srinivas, *Tripuraneni Madana Mohan;*
Viswanatha Satyanarayana, *Viswanatha Pavani Sastri.*

For Sarayu
my daughter

CONTENTS

Contents

GOD AND HIS MEANINGS

SURREALIST DETOURS

Contents

PREFACE

Every time I have written anything about Telugu for a non-Telugu audience, I have begun by saying that Telugu is the second most widely spoken language in India, spoken by about seventy million people in the southern state of Andhra Pradesh. I hope this anthology will not need such an explanatory note. Poetry stands in its own right; it does not depend on geographic and demographic support for attention. However, poetry is made of words and words are located in language. It is therefore necessary to say that Telugu is a south Indian language with a vocabulary derived from Dravidian as well as Sanskrit sources, and that it has almost a thousand years of uninterrupted literary tradition. It is a highly musical language, and all poetry was written in meter until the latter half of the twentieth century when free verse became popular.

A hundred years is a significant period in the history of any literature, even if the literature has been in existence for almost a thousand years before. The last hundred years in Telugu literature have been especially revolutionary since they witnessed events of extraordinary significance in the political and cultural history of Andhra. For one thing, Telugu came into contact with the powerful influence of English under British colonial rule. If not for the cataclysmic changes that took place in the cultural life of the country, the turn of the twentieth century in Telugu literature would have been a less eventful continuation of the new literary modes that had begun two centuries before. Depending on the worldview to which you belonged, these changes were either disruptions of a world of rich and stable creativity or a new awakening from a state that had become stagnant and deadening. In any case, the events at the turn of the century profoundly influenced every corner of Telugu life. It is my hope that this anthology will present a view of the poetry that came out of such changes as well as the diverse literary practices that flourished during the twentieth century.

But I did not intend the anthology to cover literary ideologies and movements. It is not a record of literary history with individual poets and their poems to illustrate literary periods and their contours. Such an enterprise would be interesting in itself, but I have aimed, rather, to select the best poems from the century, no matter what ideological persuasion their authors belonged to. I present a brief survey of the century's literary history as an After-Essay.

If this anthology shows anything, it is that literary value is entirely independent of any conscious purpose and is not controlled by or pigeonholed into ideas, arguments, and political practices. Poetry seeks its own argument and literary practice finds its own world, while at the same time being deeply influenced by the political, social, and ideological contexts that surround it.

During the last several decades, a heavy and even overpowering belief has emerged in the Telugu literary world that poetry has to be involved in delivering a social message and should serve as a weapon in the battle for one goal or the other. Poets have hence taken to seeing themselves as modernists rebelling against Brahminic traditions, Marxists fighting against the capitalists, militant revolutionaries battling feudal powers, feminists speaking against a male dominated society, low-caste Dalits struggling against the upper castes, minority Muslim poets standing up for their own identity, and so on. Somewhere in between, there are also pure poets imagining freedom from all contexts and "postmodernists" uninterested for the most part in communicating anything to anyone. The recent history of literature in Andhra reads like a series of polemics. Nearly every book or essay on literature pronounces a value judgment on poets based on their political opinions or social statements. Poems are evaluated for their social positions rather than for their literary quality.

This is, in fact, a healthy feature of Telugu society. Here, poetry is taken seriously; it is not just analyzed, or torn into pieces to make an arcane critical point. Nor is poetry the specialized field of professional poets and critics. It is memorized, recited and quoted in conversations. People argue about poems and the status of poets. If a public issue comes up, it is the poet who expresses what the people think and feel about it. Newspapers carry poetry and poets stand at the forefront of social or political action. To be called a poet is an honor in society, and poets are awarded, by popular acclaim, honorific titles such as *maha-kavi,* great poet, and *kavi-samrat,* king of poets. To claim a poet from their own community is the preferred means for a social group to gain upward mobility. To receive the dedication of a book of poems is an honor celebrated in public, and the release of a new book of poems is considered a newsworthy item.

For centuries Telugu poetry has been closely textured by orality. Poems are read aloud, sung, and performed. The centrality of sound has carried through despite the general rejection of meter in favor of free verse since the late 1950s. Even the printed poem, written in free verse, for the individual reader to read in the privacy of the home, continues to retain its sound value. Successful poets have always realized the complexities of sound as a means to evoke meanings beyond lexical limits.

These very features that have given health and strength to the social role of poetry in Telugu have also, not infrequently, interfered with the quality of a poem. When the dividing line between social activism and literary creativity is blurred under the overpowering influence of contemporary political and social movements, discussed in some detail in the After-Essay, literary institutions have lost their identity and merged with political parties. In the process of serving its role as public voice, poetry has, sometimes, lost its literary role. Even good poets have written bad poems just to make a public point, not to mention non-poets who have taken to poetry because it is the preferred mode of public expression.

However, it is a testament to the enduring taste of the reading public and to the quiet creative genius of the poets that good poetry continues to be written in every conceivable context, with or without political/social/communal activist orientations for the poets. Good poems receive recognition irrespective of what the poet stood for or did not stand for, and what awards he or she got or did not get. From the distance of elapsed time, it is easier to see what has lasted and what has not.

It was my good fortune that I have been closely associated with the literary scene in Telugu for the past half century and have personally known most of the poets included in this anthology, some more closely than others. My deep involvement in all the major events of Telugu literature over such a long period has given me a rich sense of the pulse and breath of Telugu poetry, but it might have also given me my biases. In literature, as in life, taste is never neutral.

I hope that the anthology will reflect the collective judgment of several generations, which has educated my taste, and that it will be received well by readers who enjoy poetry. A number of my Telugu friends will be disappointed that poems they cherish and poets they consider important are not included. I hope they will appreciate the anthology for what is here rather than reject it for what is not here. Even with all these poets covering the entire century, this is still an incomplete anthology. There are more poems to be translated and more poets to be included. A translator's work is never finished.

Now a word about translation. I confess there is a love affair between myself and the poems I have translated. If I did not love a poem, I did not translate it. If I did not feel that the poem translated well, I did not include it here. To borrow the words of American poet Charles Simic: "Translation is an actor's medium. If I cannot make myself believe that I'm writing the poem that I'm translating, no degree of aesthetic admiration for the work can help me. . . . In a successful translation, one indeed does, at times, become the Other."

"Languages are jealous sovereigns," said Rabindranath Tagore, "and passports are rarely allowed for travelers to cross their strictly guarded boundaries." Poetry is blessed by its location in the specific. It is inevitably created in a specific time, place, community, mind, dialect and language. But it acquires a new life when it crosses its boundaries. The further it moves, the longer it lives. Poetry is timeless and boundless, precisely because it is temporal and local.

ACKNOWLEDGMENTS

This anthology was built one poem at a time, over a considerable period. I had no plans of doing an anthology to begin with. I translated a poem or two for the fun of it, whenever I was bored with the day's work. In the course of time, the poems added up. Some of the poems translated easily, and some were difficult. A few were impossible, and those I abandoned. I shared the successful drafts with friends who read them and made comments. Vinay Dharwadker, who wanted some poems for an anthology of Indian poetry he was editing, read several poems and made extensive suggestions. Kirin Narayan spent several evenings watching me work on the drafts of Yenki songs, looking over my shoulder, offering the right word when I was stuck. Mary Sarko read a number of them. I still kept working on the drafts, and adding more poems. I was not sure I had an acceptable version, so I sent a copy to Carolyn Brown, then translation coordinator for the International Writing Program at University of Iowa, asking for her professional comment. All I expected from her was a word of frank opinion, whether the translations worked or not. I did not realize the amount of time she gave to the poems, until one day she came to Madison, sat with me for three days, and went through poem after poem giving careful attention to every line, and offering suggestions for a number of improvements—from major suggestions in wording, to changes in punctuation or corrections of typing errors. Every suggestion of hers was helpful to me in rethinking my drafts and I adopted many of her suggestions. If I still persisted in keeping what I wrote in a few places, it was my stubborn Telugu sensibility. I cannot thank Carolyn enough for the attention she gave these poems. I kept working on the translations adding more poems as I worked. During the

summer of 1999, I had the opportunity to read some of these trans-
lations with David Shulman in Jerusalem. He suggested a number of
changes and also read my After-Essay with great care. Christopher
Chekuri's questions forced me to rewrite my After-Essay at a stage
when I thought I had finished it, by bringing to my attention how
much I took for granted from my readers. At different stages in the
making of the drafts, when each one looked almost final, I gave the
poems and the After-Essay to Sylvia Dakessian for editing. She went
through every comma and semicolon. I deeply appreciate her sensitive
reading of the drafts.

Some years ago, I translated a few poems of Revati Devi and Jaya-
prabha with A. K. Ramanujan for the Oxford Anthology of Modern
Indian Poetry that he and Vinay Dharwadker edited. Later, I translated
some poems from Viswanatha Satyanarayana's *Krishna Sangitamu* with
David Shulman. They were my favorite poems; I include them here. I
only wish I had David's company in working on all of these poems.

Pillalamarri Ramulu of Hyderabad, searched for copies of poetry
publications unavailable to me in Madison. Attaluri Narasimharao of
Visakhapatnam supplied information about poets, their dates of birth
and other such details not found in published sources. Chalasani Prasad
helped me with dates on Sri Sri's works. Pemmaraju Venugopala Rao,
Veluri Venkateswara Rao, Jampala Chawdary, K. V. S. Ramarao, Sari-
palli Kanaka Prasad, and a number of my other friends in the Telugu
community in the United States have helped me with their advice and
support.

Phyllis Granoff and Wendy Doniger were very supportive of the
project, and offered helpful comments.

Working on Telugu poetry from Madison was, at times, a very lonely
task. There was no one to talk to, no one who knew these poems
anywhere near. Chekuri Ramarao always listened to my long and not
always coherent thoughts on the poems I was working on whenever I
called him from Madison at such times that were convenient for me,
but were his late nights or early mornings in Hyderabad. That he always
listened to me, and offered his gentle, informed advice was an irrefut-
able proof of his love of Telugu poetry and his warm friendship.

The work that I began in Madison was completed in the gentle and quiet atmosphere of the Wissenschaftskolleg zu Berlin. A fellowship from the Kolleg has given me the crucial time I needed to reflect on the translations and finalize the drafts. My friends David Shulman and Sanjay Subrahmanyam, who were at the Kolleg with me, have created an atmosphere of sustained warmth and support. Paruchuri Srinivas was my walking bibliography. Conveniently stationed not too far from Berlin, he listened to my questions on my late night telephone calls, day after day and patiently answered them. Vakulabharanam Rajagopal promptly attended to my demands for information by locating precisely what I needed from the books in University of Wisconsin's Memorial Library, and Terri Wipperfurth kept track of my correspondence during my absence from Madison.

All this work would not have seen the light of day if C. Dharmarao from Hyderabad had not taken upon himself the huge responsibility of collecting the copyright permissions from all the poets or their heirs, many of whom were not even easy to locate. Needless to add that I owe my thanks to all of the poets and their heirs who gave me their permission to use the material they hold copyrights on and especially to Saroja Sri Sri who graciously facilitated the release of the copyright on Sri Sri's poems.

Last but not least, the Telugu Association of North America (TANA), through its Publication Committee, supported the publication of this book through a subvention. It is a pleasure to thank them for it, and Gangadhar Nadella and Jampala Chowdary for making it possible.

A NOTE ON
TELUGU NAMES

Telugu names are usually in three parts. The first part is the family name, which shares some of the functions of the last name of European and American names; the second part is the given name, which could have several components to it making it very long; and the last part is the caste title (e.g., Reddy, Sastri, Raju, and so on). During the twentieth century, this slot is taken over by names such as Rao, Babu, and Baba, which have no connotation of caste and are used as part of the given name. Women may have only two parts in their names, the family name followed by the given name, which may carry an extension to it, such as Devi or Amma. Christian names follow the same order—family name, given name—except that the given name is often a Biblical name. However, Muslim names carry their family name at the end, as the last part of their name. A feature of modernity is that many poets have adopted pen names, which have replaced all their other names in their publications.

In writing the names of the poets, I adopted the style the particular poet used in his or her publications. The notes give the names in alphabetical order, in exactly the same style as they appear with the poems. However, if the name used by a poet is different from their full name, I give the full name in the biographical notes.

GUIDE TO
PRONUNCIATION

No diacritics are used in the body of the poems. No diacritics are used for the names of modern authors. Diacritics, however, are used in the notes to indicate the pronunciation of Telugu words and Sanskrit, Urdu, and English words assimilated into Telugu. Original titles of poems and books, as well as names of premodern authors, are given with diacritics.

Long vowels are double the length of short vowels and are marked with a macron. The Sanskrit diphthongs *e, o, ai,* and *au* are always long and are unmarked; we mark the short Dravidian vowels *ĕ* and *ŏ*. Sanskrit names ending in a long vowel, appearing in Telugu texts, are consistently marked as short, in keeping with Telugu practice: Sita < Sitā, Draupadi < Draupadī.

ṭ, ḍ, ṭh, ḍh, ṇ, and *ḷ* are retroflex, pronounced by turning the tip of the tongue back toward the palate. *ṅ* is a palatal nasal and *ñ* is a velar nasal.

A NOTE ON THE TRANSLATIONS

"Born for Poetry" by Chellapilla Venkata Sastri; "The Beginning" and "Song of Krishna" by Viswanatha Satyanarayana; and "The Farmer's Song" and "A Longing" by Abburi Ramakrishna Rao were translated with David Shulman.

"Some People Laugh / Some People Cry" and "Myth of Myself" by Sri Sri; "We Write" by Siva Reddy; and "This Night," "The Voice," "God," and "This World, Poor Thing" by Revati Devi were translated with A. K. Ramanujan.

LANGUAGES OF POETRY

To create delight, you have to know the world.

Born for Poetry

～ CHELLAPILLA VENKATA SASTRI

I was born for poetry.
Making good poems is my business.
That's how I'll cross to the other shore.
All my fortune comes from poetry.
I've conquered death, and I'll defeat old age.

If anyone faults my poetry, even my teacher,
even God himself, I'll fight back
and win.

Biographical information about the poets and notes to the poems begin on page 241.

The Other Tongue

∽ DASU SRIRAMULU

The village elders gather on the porch of the Rama temple
to recite the *Mahabharata* and talk of other things.

"Telugu is a good language," they say.
"This hissing-spitting *Engilis* that our boys are speaking
goes no farther than their lips
even if they pass F. A., B. A., or some other A."

The Comet

A string of pearls is what I make
choosing lucid words.
I'll combine old with something new
to create a new poem.

You say you don't like it.
Who cares? Go
play with your wooden dolls.
You don't want a living woman.

2

It was early in the morning.
The comet and the morning star
arrived in the sky to serve
their master, Light of Day.

The stars were drowned in light.
Darkness fled the sky.
Somewhere a single *koil*
sang from a faraway tree.

The cock crowed its morning call.
The flowers opened their eyes.
Now and then a light breeze
gently moved the leaves.

The Comet

I had just returned from the city
after a couple of days' visit.
I talked with those experts
who work for social change.

I came home and woke up my wife.
"Look up at the sky," I said,
"that's the Arrow of Desire shining.
See how brilliant it looks from here."

Startled awake, she saw
neither me nor the sky at first.
She quickly fixed her hair and sash,
and was very cross with me.

"The moon doesn't want to meet
the Dragon's Tail among planets.
Your face doesn't want to look
at this Tail of Smoke in the sky.

But it's not a tail of smoke.
It's a lily of silver light.
Gods give this as a gift
to women they dearly love.

A luminous thing of beauty
whenever it appears in our sky—
small minds from a dead past
think it brings them evil.

This ornament the gods made
doesn't bring any evil.
It adds new color to the sky
hanging from above.

Poets make up things
good, bad, and indifferent.
Scholars do not trust
any of their crazy myths.

The English people know.
They see what the eye can't see.
Taught by them I've learned
the truth of things as they are.

This comet is a relative
of the earth. He comes to visit
the terrestrial neighborhood
every once in awhile.

What's the point in thinking
that this comet causes evil?
I believe it actually is
a harbinger of change.

The magic of words will break
the chains of caste and race.
Together we will thrive
not so long from now.

All the world will be one.
Caste will soon be a lie.
Love will bind us together
in a single happiness.

Religions will not divide us.
Knowledge alone will shine.
Pleasures promised in heaven—
we'll have them here on earth.

The other day in the city
the wise men held a dinner
for all castes together—
that was the first step."

I finished my story.
My wife didn't say a word.
After a while she spoke
with tears in her eyes.

3

"I've heard about your ways.
I'm worried about you.
You're humiliating your wife.
And you think you're doing great?

My friends sneer at me.
The neighbors console me.
How can I bear those women
who just laugh at me?

Your father's very sad;
he thinks the times are bad.
Your mother probably believes
I am in it with you.

Enough of your games now.
Is this what English teaches?
If your elders had known this,
they would never have sent you to school.

They wanted you to be a Raja.
That's why they sent you to college.

Learning, meant for a living
has shaken the roots of life.

Never mind the wife.
You don't have to care for her.
But what about your parents,
who raised and cared for you?

For unity of caste and race
you need more than a meal.
Why don't you go and marry
an untouchable woman, I say."

Upset and angry,
she threw her pearls at me
and walked away in fury
like lightning in the sky.

The day has fully dawned
and the comet has disappeared.
Don't people know what's good
and what, in their world, is bad?

The Beginning

First Verses from the *Ramayana*

∾ VISWANATHA SATYANARAYANA

Lord of the worlds:
you are the treasure of wholeness, perfection of rest,
unfolding joy, white peak of awareness
and threshold of freedom.
You are the light that sees me, the only one
I serve.

The five elements, sun and moon, are your
seven bodies, so this body
is yours. I open my eyes,
I close them: this means you exist.
If this body has a Master, he is you.
That makes eight. What is left
that is me, except a name I call "me"?
This whole world can't know you
although it is only you,
for it can't see the light behind
its eyes.

Brahma knows only a quarter,
and Parvati knows only half.
You know Rama in his fullness.
With your permission, Lord,
I will dedicate this story of Rama,

husband of Sita,
to you.

Waking, dreaming, and in deep sleep,
my mind and my tongue says Rama's name.
But like a horse, my mind goes
every which way, unbridled
by the story. You, lord, are strong:
you are the driver.
Take the reins in your hand.

"If you want to write,
write the story of Rama.
What do you get but needless trouble
from made-up stories? They're good neither
for this world nor the next."
My father's command and my own anguish
became one. I will write the story
of Rama, the one story equal to
the wonder of thought.

If you ask, "Why yet *another* Ramayana?"
my answer is: In this world,
everyone eats the same rice every day,
but the taste of *your* life is your own.
People make love, over and over, but only you
know how it feels. I write about the same Rama
everyone else has known, but my feelings of love
are mine. Ninety percent of what makes a poem
is the genius of the poet. Poets in India know
that the way you tell the tale

weighs a thousand times more
than some novel theme.

When the Twin Poets, Tirupati and Venkata Sastri,
were storming the country with poetry, I went to Bandar
to study English. There I became a student of Venkata Sastri
and, drinking at the source, bathing in his words,
I became a poet.

His heart is gentle. Gentler still
is every poem he writes. The love he feels
for his students is gentle beyond words.
To claim Chellapilla Venkana,
a terror to his enemies,
as my teacher
is a matter of pride
in this Telugu land.

Nannayya did not have such luck.
Neither did Tikkana.
Only Chellapilla Venkana has had the good fortune
of having someone like me
as his student, who has taken in
the goddess of speech in all her wisdom
and inner strength and newness. I'll fill the skies
with the soft light of his fame.

I remember Kodali Anjaneyulu, who deserted poetry,
his beloved, whose every word is a precious gem,
and joined the swordless army of the Mahatma
in the battle beyond violence. He was my friend
and partner in poetry.

If he had stayed with me, we would have poured out
poetry like blocks of candied sugar, like Potana himself.

My mind is too fast, like the arc
of a burning torch. It won't tolerate
a break, or pause even for a second
to choose a word.

Mine is the language people use. My style
is deep. I aim at delight and meaning.
To create delight, you have to know the world.
There's no poetry without the world.

Call of Poetry

ༀ SRI SRI

When I was young,
when dreams of my youth blossomed like melodies newly sung,
I adored poetry.
She was a beauty beyond reach
riding above the clouds
in a gorgeous palanquin
far away.

My search for poetry
was a longing, a penance—
every minute
a rush.

But no matter where I looked,
I saw a forest of figures of speech
and word games
pretending to be poetry.
There were days I sat alone
in my cave, in my hut, in my own darkness
languishing for poetry.

Then under the power of my worlds,
with long dedication, learning and discipline,
in my stillness of oneness,
in my mind that opened like the gateway to heaven,
what noises, languages, what views I saw!

What worlds of colors ever new and newer!
My song gained life from what sources of energy!
And what sounds I chose for my poem!

Wherever I searched, I heard
heaps of sounds, sounds that call,
sounds of the conch and drum
from the deep of the ocean—
an ocean that is shaken by a wild tempest
in the middle of the night
by torrents of rain from all the sky.

That very night I heard
all the animals of the forests crying, defying rhythm,
all the music hidden deep inside the stars,
earthquakes
falling governments
revolutions
war
all of them forms of poetic energy—
the world vision of poetry!

And what did I see when I thought of poetry?
And what did I hear for its commentary?

A diamond blossoming on top of fire.
A flying iron horse.
And the drumming of cannon fire
sounding like high fever.

What else did I hear?

The thoughts whirling in the mind
of a young mother who just gave birth—

her delicious dreams with her child in her lap.
And the sounds of primal memories
that lulled the infant to sleep.

The blood flowing in the veins of the patient
on the boundary between life and death—
on the operating table.

The drivel of the drunk
who dozes in the gutter—
he cannot even move.

The cruel rape of the hungry whore
and the refrain of pain in her half-closed eyes.

The secrets the hanged head revealed.

An owl's hoot and a frog's croak
in the moonless night
of an insane mind.

The hunger and pain
of the workers on strike,
of the wives and children of the workers on strike.

Words of a million stars.
Songs of a billion waterfalls
and the roar of a hundred billion ocean waves.

I heard them all.

I looked for words to say it all
and they came in battalions
crossing dead dictionaries
breaking the shackles of grammar

free from the serpentine embrace of meter.
They came running
and entered my heart.

In that whirlwind of words
a rush of the river of revolution
what paths I traversed
what music I made!
Cleansed of all my sins
what waves of joy lifted me!
My senses fully awake
what was I composing, was I alive,
awake, seeing, breathing
or had I entered
nirvana!

I was enchanted by that music,
music from stars making love,
the kiss of joy and the sounds of life—
born at the very moment of the end of life,
sounds of music of many many worlds
that hold the body in the tight embrace of the rising phoenix
in a state beyond pleasure and pain—
beyond thought, beyond knowing,
unfathomable, pure.

The music was me,
one with me.
It was momentary, eternal.
It was poetry.

When I was in my mother's womb,
when my self was just taking shape,
life was beginning in all my senses.
I fell to this earth,

accepted pleasure and pain
through life's journey
in fear
when something took me by hand,
rained its compassion on me,
compassion incomparable,
endless.
It was poetry.

Today,
do you hear my breathless thoughts,
the adventures of my imagination!

Whatever I write
reflects this world and my dedication to the world.
My song shall come from my heart
and it shall be the song of my people.
My sky shall be closer to the earth
and my dreams shall be a shower of light that all my brothers may
share equally.
The words I make
within my reach but beyond the bounds
will form the temple I build for poetry.
My song shall be an offering at the altar of poetry
to the joy that is poetry,
mother poetry.

The Buried Poem

ISMAIL

The poet digs deep for the poem
it's buried under tons of mud
tons of mind
it's buried in so deep
it'll take days and nights
to pull the coffin out

It will live
if there's a little breath left
maybe

But every time he digs up the coffin
the body that comes out of it alive
is himself

Poetry

∾ ISMAIL

A beautiful woman
came to me
put a seed in my palm
and walked away
without a word

I will sow this seed
and nurse the plant
until it grows
into a great big tree
that spreads its branches
to the end of space

Then I will climb
the limb that extends into the sunrise
and go thousands of miles
searching for her

First Blood

∽ VEGUNTA MOHANA PRASAD

Somewhere
a girl
sees her first blood
under the shadows of oleander trees
and gets scared

The poet keeps vigil all night
blows his horn fearfully alone
pulling his blanket tight in the cold
waiting for a new morning
and he dies at dawn
No one sheds a tear for him

No one consoles
the girl on her first blood

The poet squeezes the darkness
all night
fills his throat with the grief
of the world
No one is startled
at the foam thrown up
in his last breath

Liberation

~ VEGUNTA MOHANA PRASAD

All this time is spent around paper
writing on paper
reading what you wrote in books
waiting wide-eyed for someone
to bring a new book
reading without sleep
all this time is spent around paper

Every single tear is a dead corpse
I bury it burn it on a handful of paper
I wake up from sleep and cry for peace
in my sleepless heart of deep death
All this time is spent in tearful books

Whose bones are these, whose
are these sound waves of skulls?
A sudden rain of nerves asks as it
tears up each layer of darkness
strikes lightning like hunger

Fires of grief, of expressionist
individualistic grief are put out
from my desert mind

Hungry intestines entangle
my feet
All this time is spent in tearful paper

Rain sharp like needles
shrill like crickets
rain all night
I roast my heart like corn on the cob
on the fires I kindled in my head

The paper I wrote on
is drenched in the sharp rain
of nerves and needles
gets soaking wet
and sheds tears again

For peace of mind
or world peace?

Don't know

HUSBANDS, LOVERS, WIVES, AND WOMEN

*They are poems
that sparkle
with a beauty you've never known,
and will never fully understand.*

Gold

A conversation between a husband and wife, circa 1910

∾ GURAJADA APPARAO

"What were we fighting about?
I forgot. Don't laugh at me.
Listen.
There are two kinds of riches.
One grows from the earth, the other
from the heart.
It's rare that both occur together.
Which of the two should women want?"

"Is there such a thing as wealth of the heart?
I thought gold is the only kind."

"Even the wise fall for gold.
No wonder it dazzles women.
Gold gives you beauty
like flowers on a vine.
But only love has fragrance.
Without it
a woman's beauty looks wooden.

You use turmeric on your body.
Comb your hair. Wear flowers.
Put mascara on your eyes.
Your lips are red with betel
and your teeth are shining.
You look beautiful.

Gold

Love doesn't grow by itself either.
You love and you are loved.
You give love to get love.

You give me that look as if to say:
'Do you eat love?
What is it anyway? I don't know if I have it in me.'

Love is everything.
But parents don't teach
this art at home.
Teachers don't either.
The texts are silent about it.
Thanks to poets
I learned it.
I brought you a heart full of love
like a precious diamond.
Take it.

You ask me, 'How do I wear it?'
But you already have.
Look at yourself
with *my* eyes.

A loving husband brings sunlight
so you blossom
like a flower.

Without love
life is dark.

You think I tricked you with a poem
instead of giving a real gift?
This poem is pure gold
when you lend your ears to it.

Husband is an old word.
I am your friend,
poor without your love.
But if I have it, I'm
richer than the king of gods."

Chained

∾ RAYAPROLU SUBBARAO

No one was at the door
when that young woman chained my hands
with a strand of white *ponna* flowers.
God was my only witness.

In her sweet voice she said:
Promise me, with your hand in mine,
you will never break this.

I cannot break the flowers, I will
bear them until the string slips
from my hand
growing thin.

Waiting

RAYAPROLU SUBBARAO

Sandal paste dry in the golden bowl.
Garlands hang from the door frame.
Bath oil seeps into the grinding stone.
Young woman! Who are you waiting for?

The part in your hair is disheveled.
Your braid has fallen loose.
You don't even fix the dot on your forehead.
Woman, who stole your heart?

You can't contain your passion
rising like boiling milk.
Who did you lose your heart to,
on this evening of new rains?

The Palanquin

∽ DEVULAPALLI KRISHNA SASTRI

When my lover sent his palanquin for me
my heart shivered in joy.
My body, withered from our separation,
flowered
like a tree in spring.

With shaking hands
I put on my dress.
My garments of cloud.
My ornaments of dawn.

It was a happiness that burnt me.
It was a heaviness that made me light.
Whatever the feeling was
it was beyond me to bear it.

I softly walked to the palanquin and sat.
A garland among flowers in bloom.

When the bearers chanted O *oho*,
village after village lined the streets.

As the bearers chanted O *oho*,
the path woke up at the edge of the village.

The bearers chanted O *oho*,
the stream dozed at the end of the garden.

The palanquin
is my song of love,
a vine heavy with flowers.
My palanquin
is the rainbow's arc,
a tree
of springtime dreams.

Her Eyes

～ DEVULAPALLI KRISHNA SASTRI

Her eyes have in them
dark shadows from an endless sky.

In places you see
hues of sleep
from the depths of a calm, clear pond.

Sometimes you hear in them
murmurs of darkness that hide at the end of day
in crooked paths
that meander through the *nipa* leaves.

At other times
tears from monsoon clouds
hide in her eyes.

They are poems
that sparkle
with a beauty you've never known,

and will never fully understand.

In Search of Krishna

‿ DEVULAPALLI KRISHNA SASTRI

"Are you
a gentle ray of moonlight
visiting the earth
sliding through the narrow paths of fresh leaves?
Or a vine covered with flowers?
Who are you, young woman,
all alone
among the *nipa* trees?

It's dark and you can't see anything.
The heavy clouds
pour darkness all around.
Where are you going in the dead of night?
Your wide dark eyes only thicken the darkness,
and your hot sighs wake
the very air from sleep."

"It was an autumn night.
The entire village was sleeping
on the silver bed of moonlight.
Every cowherd
and every cowherdess.

We made love
and I was lying
in my husband's soft embrace,
in a deep sleep

beyond joy, beyond pain,
wandering free in the world of dreams,
when I was awakened by the gentle sounds of the flute
mingled with the river's music
moving across the sky,
all white in moonlight.

Like a flower's desire floating on the song of the bee,
a slender leaf-boat sailing on a river of jasmine honey,
a cuckoo's call afloat on the first morning breeze,
a wisp of white cloud awash in the soft flood of moonlight,
a gentle rain, a soft drizzle,
a running rivulet, an ocean wave
touching the edge of the sky,

that music flowed from the flute.
My heart was lost in melody.

I ran with it,
my heart ran faster.
I forgot myself, forgot everything,
forgot it was night."

"You never left before
the arms of the man who held you,
never left your home and village.
A wild forest,
the middle of the night—
how, just how, were you able
to go?"

"The gentle breeze fragrant with music,
sweet with honeyed sounds,
the waves breaking on the banks of Yamuna,
pounding like so many drums—

they showed me the way.
My passion hastened me
and I went.

See how the river keeps calling him with its failing voice.
Look at that sandbank, it lies lifeless and pale.
I ran here on this path no one had ever gone before.
Look at these trees: they lift their empty hands and gaze
aimlessly, far and wide.

He sat right here, and I, here.
I was here, under this *jaji* vine
and he was beneath this *kadimi* tree.
I can see it all as if it were happening now,
before my eyes.

The bright light of the autumn moon,
the dark breeze from the flowing river
this *nipa* branch swayed by the gentle midnight wind
and I, the faint gopi,
—we all heard the maddening music of his flute.

If a gust of wind embraces it,
that young bamboo opens up and sings.
When the man who makes the world fall in love with him
touches his lips to it,
can you imagine what it can do?

We've never known a singer
like the young Krishna.
What he plays is
not just the flute in his hand.
He can make my dried-up heart,
my broken life,
play with joy.

In Search of Krishna

In the flow of melodies from the flute,
in the hands of Nanda's son,
in that pouring stream,
the moon
and all the stars
melt and merge
like so many strands of song.

Have you ever seen that man,
have you ever seen the curve of his smile,
the glances from his black eyes
and the lock of hair on his brow
moving in the wind?

The dancing peacock feather on his head
as he plays his flute—
that young man—have you ever seen him?

No more moonlit nights,
no more garlands of light,
no more waves dancing on the river,
no more hairs standing on end,
no more songs for me
by the young cowherd Krishna.

The bee's song the jasmine has saved
in the heart of its tender silk petals,
the spring's music captured by the bird
as the season slips out of sight,
the sound of the sea the river remembers
as she separates for her ocean lover,
the lyric of moonlight in the eyes of the star
that searches for her lunar lord:

This is Krihsna's music in my heart.
I am searching for the one who makes that music,
the young man who makes
the world fall in love with him.

This is my story.
You listen, you're startled, you tremble.
You are looking for something with your darting eyes.
Who are you, young woman
among the *nipa* trees?"

He Didn't Come Back

〜 NANDURI SUBBARAO

Moon, he didn't come back.
My friend you met that day got angry and left.

Yenki, just you and me—no one else—he said.
These fields and gardens,
they're all yours, he said.

You want to go? Am I boring you
with my story?

This day is ours forever, he said.
I won't touch another,
not even the wind, he said.

You're laughing at me, Moon,
that's not fair.

He looked at me
and looked at you.
The Moon is our witness, he said.

I didn't want to make you sad.
I just wanted to tell you.

Moon, he didn't come back.

Blow Out the Lamp

∾ NANDURI SUBBARAO

Blow out the lamp.
My mind can't hold you in the light.

I want the garden totally dark.
I want to see your eyes shine.

Blow out the lamp.
My mind can't hold you in the light.

I will think of your beauty over and over
peering until I see all of you.

Blow out the lamp.
My mind can't hold you in the light.

We'll stop looking and forget form
and fall asleep unaware of each other.

Blow out the lamp.
My mind can't hold you in the light.

The Farmer's Song

∾ ABBURI RAMAKRISHNA RAO

Come, spring is young
in the shade of the blossoming mango.
Hand in hand we'll go smiling and singing
to forget our thoughts,
right into the fragrance.

You've put the ropes and the milking pots there,
ready for the cows when they're driven home
at sunset. You sit there shyly—and I long to play,
to swing, you and I, under the trees
with no one as far as you can see.

If you don't want to sing, don't even look
at the river, at the boats that are sailing.
We'll sit at the edge of the fields
behind the trees, our bodies touching,
and say nothing, two crows on a branch.

You in My Dream

∾ NANDURI SUBBARAO

Don't wake me up from this sleep.
Yenki, don't.
I've never known pleasure like this.

Yenki is telling stories in my dream
and I'm listening, amazed
at every twist.

Don't wake me up, Yenki, don't.

She's the teller, she's in the tale.
Every turn's magical.
What a story she makes!

Don't wake me up, Yenki, don't.

She flies like a bird
moves like a star
laughs like a flower
she's new every minute.

Don't wake me up, Yenki, don't.

You in My Dream

Don't let me wake up.
The dream melts away.
To you, I am one.
To me, you are many.

Don't wake me up, Yenki, don't.

My Love

~ NANDURI SUBBARAO

"Who were we in our past life?"
Yenki became shy and giggled.

"What will be our future life?"
She turned pale, amazed.

"How long will our happiness last?"
Tears in her eyes, she grew sad.

Tryst

∾ DUVVURI RAMIREDDY

In the middle of the night
you go to meet your lover,
softly,
as if walking on air.

You hold your anklets in your hand
so they don't make a sound.

When the owl hoots from his midnight nest,
you look over your shoulder, scared.

You are startled at your own footsteps,
and cry, "Who's that?"

In your white dress
and your light skin,
no one can see you
in the flood of moonlight.

But the fragrance of your body—
it spreads where you walk.
Girl,
how do you disguise that?

Is This All!

∾ NANDURI SUBBARAO

Is this all!
The ocean is so small.
It only fills the little space
between us and the sun, that's all!

When my own people talked
of me and my morals,
my pain, you said, was huge like the ocean.

Is this all!
The ocean is so small!

When my man looked at me
as if I was not his woman,
my heart, you said, moaned like the ocean.

Is this all!
The ocean is so small!

When I held my baby, who knows the truth,
I cried, you said, an ocean of tears.

Is this all!
The ocean is so small!

Is This All!

When you said it has no end, no shore,
and it holds eternal life,
I thought it was big—
big like God.

Is this all!

You on My Mind

∾ KAVIKONDALA VENKATARAO

With you on my mind I walked away
tearing up flowers, crushing buds.

I didn't think of the possible fruit.
I didn't think of savoring the honey.

I watched the foam by the edge of the ocean,
watched the waves make little bubbles.
But I never thought of diving in
to catch the wealth of pearls in the deep.

With you on my mind I walked away
tearing up flowers, crushing buds.

I hoped to reach the twinkling star,
its tiny light on the top of the hill.
I failed to see the candle held
next to me, so easy to reach.

With you on my mind I walked away
tearing up flowers, crushing buds.

You

∾ ISMAIL

You're mine
only when you take off all your clothes
for me

When you're dressed
you belong to the world

I'm going to shred this world
into pieces
one day

Going out of Town

༄ REVATI DEVI

The train's going to that town.
Me sitting in the train,
am I going to the same town?

The ant crawling from one end to the other
in this car—where is it going?
From the far side of the earth,
the train's no different.

Leaning against the window
resting my chin on it—
the train isn't moving.
I'm not moving.
The trees and houses alongside
race the other way.

My mind's racing with them.

Those smiling eyes still on my lips,
that warm heart still in my heart—

I didn't go anywhere.
Not even for a second.

Hibiscus on the Lake

∾ CHAVALI BANGARAMMA

The plant saw the beauty of water,
the flowering plant with bright red flowers.
She told me all about water.

Bending over the water to put on her *bottu,*
she saw the beauty of water.

I watched the loveliness,
until I fainted.
Snakes like trees ran through the lake.

The plant saw the beauty of water,
the flowering plant with bright red flowers.

The sky saw it all.
It trembled in fear
and fell down on the banks.
The sun went up the tree
too scared to look.

The plant saw the beauty of water,
the flowering plant with bright red flowers.
She spread out her hair.
Her *bottu* fell off.
The banks shed tears
and the shore was shaken.

The plant with bright red flowers,
bending, still bending
told me of the beauty of water.

The hibiscus talked to me.

Invocation

∾ REVATI DEVI

Why you? Even I didn't think I could write anything at all.
Let alone poetry.

Sometime,
yesterday, the day before, sometime ago or sometime now
when I fall into an abyss of sadness
when I lose myself in the heights of love
when I float on the white clouds of joy
sometime like that
when he becomes me,
except then—

never mind poetry,
I didn't think I could write anything at all.
Let alone you.

A Letter

KAVIKONDALA VENKATARAO

The mail runner carries the bag of mail.
The bells on his spear ring.
Why does the sound echo in my heart
when I meet him on my way?
Why do my feet get confused
and quicken to run—as he runs?

I am not carrying a bag of mail,
so, why do I gasp for breath?
Strange this life,
maybe it is
carrying a letter to someone.

My Brother

∾ CHAVALI BANGARAMMA

When my brother talks to me
my mind opens like jasmine.
He is the sky—
he looks at me from there.
I am the earth,
and I look at him from here.

When we call each other brother, sister,
it sounds like lightning
to everyone else.

The dazzling looks he shoots at me,
I take them in with a shiver of joy.
I speak my grief with him.
He tells me of his own.

I give his feelings
to all the world.
But to speak of our love there are no words.
He is the brother you don't have.

An Act of Caution

~ MAHE JABEEN

I am determined to continue this bond

no, not with fire as our witness

we slept under that tree
the sky our witness
the earth our witness
the seven seas our witness
the seasons our witness
the new moon our witness
the moon of the fifth day our witness

we walked all over the green forest

when we cancel all distance
a final presence remains—
he and I

silence talks
looks touch

I am always alert before him
I assume a serious posture
of caution in my words

An Act of Caution

my face becomes a flat field of no feelings
my eyes ready to shoot at sight
but somewhere something goes wrong
a smile escapes from me
captivating

Van Gogh's Ear

~ ISMAIL

For the love of his girlfriend,
for the love of the world,
van Gogh cut off his ear
and glued it to the sky.

Since then
it puts out
a little blood,
a few tears,
a little sunshine,
and a little shade.

The reins of the horse carts
that run on the paths of
Wassenaarse gardens
come out of van Gogh's ear
every afternoon.

The circles and tunnels
of the canals of Amsterdam
that cut the melodies of light and shade
into thin strips
attach them together
and cut them again
and flow as pure waves of sound—

Van Gogh's Ear

they are actually from
van Gogh's ear.

This boy was sitting in his dark room
digging into the roots of darkness.
Why does the sun shine
only on one side of the room?
He wanted sunshine on both sides.
He had to cut off van Gogh's other ear
and hang it on this side of the sky.
He ran to the van Gogh museum.
But even before he cut off the ear
the guards overpowered him.

That's why sun shines
only on one side of the wall.

Author's Consent

∾ MAHE JABEEN

right then
as poetry happens
he comes and
kisses me

trying to find meter
in the sound of his feet
I close my eyes

youth
engulfs me
thoughts
that were taking shape
lose their way
my poetic images
get mercilessly plundered

an unmasked love
kisses my naked forehead
a touch immersed in my eyes
shines provocatively
on my cheek
a look perches on the curve of my neck
and moves like a breeze

Author's Consent

poetry freed from words
entwines us

lips publish the poem
with the author's consent

Distance

How much farther? Not much farther.
How much farther? Not much farther.

We sang the rhyme in childhood
when we did not know
what distance was.

We walked till we were tired
but did not know distance—we knew
only that we were tired.

A distance that can only talk status
between us and the neighbors.

A friendless distance of bronze walls
between mind and mind.

A distance of generations
between parents and children
like layers of asphalt.

Between people and people
a distance of civilized cities—
hidden by light.

Distance

Between this person and that person
a distance of differences—
conflicts.

Between the child and the unwed mother
a distance of dark speechless agony.

Between husband and wife
a distance of circles
that bullocks travel
hitched to an oil press.

Only bodies have no distance.
Give a rupee
or tie the thread.
That will bring bodies close.

A Suggestion

ISMAIL

we can't play these roles anymore

the role of wife
and the role of husband

let's fly away
like cotton seeds

Relationships

∿ MAHE JABEEN

The earth continues to be round.
Time stays as it has been.
Civilization, uncivil as usual.
There's nothing other than woman to talk about
in the street corners of life.
The world here goes around women
and sex.

How did you write that love story?
Who's the man in that poem?
Questions.

I leave their questions
their worries
in their care and walk away.
A crowd of feelings tangle my feet.

One man is an artist,
the other, a singer.
One is a movement,
the other, a line.
That one is a poet, this one is a sculptor.
One is all mind, the other has a heart.
I don't want to lose anyone.
I don't feel like walking away from
anything.

I find what I want
between person and person.
I keep walking
under the endless sky
carrying dreams.

Beauty ahead of me.

Nothing Happened

∾ SMILE

We're through with making love, right?
Now we need the world.

I look around idly.
My groans, vulgar words, our nothings
move like the geckos
on the wall.

Funny, isn't it?

My half-naked body
whirls round and round
in the shining steel eye
of the ceiling fan.

She turns to the wall,
putting on her sari.
Maybe they aren't shy
about showing their back.

We made love, right?
Now we need the world.

She opens the door a crack,
as if we kept it that way for ages
for the breeze.
She opens the windows wide,

invites the sky, the light, and its smells
and combs her hair,
looking casually into the mirror.

She combs her hair
like nothing happened,
really nothing happened.
Like we never heard the noises of kids
playing in the street below
on a holiday afternoon.

Cold Meat

∾ REVATI DEVI

The equator's hot
hotter than hot.
Dogs in heat go
like dogs.

The rhetoric of relations
keeps you warm.

But my heart's colder
than a corpse in a morgue.
It's a piece of meat, cold as ice.
The fire it needs

to melt
burns the world to ashes—
they fear.

This heart remains
a pyre
that never burns.

GOD AND HIS MEANINGS

Not just I, the whole world
sings that very song

Your Chariot

~ VISWANATHA SATYANARAYANA

Lord,
your chariot sped along
given to reckless speed, and my body
was crushed under it—blood gushed out in rivulets.

Dazzling, luminous, your chariot didn't stop
to see what this bump was.
Didn't even look back
at my sudden dying cry.

Tomorrow
your charioteer will clean
my blood off the wheels. But, lord,

from the millions of bloodstains
marking the wheels,
how will you know
which was mine?

The Blind Beggar

∾ VISWANATHA SATYANARAYANA

Every time I go by the train
he boards it at some place.
His daughter follows him, helping him walk.

He always sings the same poem
from the *Hundred for Rama.*

His voice is the same
as in a previous life.
He was dying in an abandoned well—
there was no one around,
he called and called
for help.
His voice grew weaker and weaker,
caught between breath and throat.

It must have found him again in this life
after a long search.

His eyes are the same dry sockets.
He was peering out from the well
hoping someone would come to save him.
He stood, a last glimmer of life in his eyes.
Those eyes found him again
in this life.

As I listen to his song
and look at his eyes,
my mind rushes to save him
from drowning in that well.

He stops his song,
asks the passengers for coins
and leaves—
his daughter leading him.

And I'm
left there.

A Longing

◠ ABBURI RAMAKRISHNA RAO

Not just I, the whole world
sings that very song

with the heaviness of despair,
in the many tones of love.

From deep inside the worlds—
a cry for help, a longing
to touch

the feet of God.

Steps

∿ ADIVI BAPIRAJU

steps
steps
rock steps
dark black
rock steps

up they go
up they lead
to lands unknown
paths unseen

steps
steps
rock steps
dark black
rock steps

millions of feet
walked on them
wore them down
wore them smooth

steps
steps
rock steps
dark black
rock steps

Steps

small feet
young feet
little feet
big feet
harsh
soft
loving feet
giving feet
sinner's feet
saint's feet

hundreds of years
millions of feet
wore them down
wore them thin

steps
steps
rock steps
dark black
rock steps

silver anklets
jingling bells
toe rings
foot strings
chiming
ringing
one by one
climbing feet
flowing feet

steps
steps
rock steps

dark black
rock steps

up they go
up they lead
to lands unknown
paths unseen

to gods up there
up above
far above

steps
steps
rock steps
dark black
rock steps

Song of Krishna

❧ VISWANATHA SATYANARAYANA

"I agree with everything you say. He's a five-year-old boy, maybe six, at most. Fall in love with him? He's a sweet little fellow and you've fallen for his music, that's all. Fine. But in another ten years, he'll come of age. Will you be able to stay away from him then? You'll be used to it. He'll want you, and you won't be able to say no.

You say by then you'll be too old. Actually, all you women will be thirty or so, in the prime of your youth.

You say he'll be married by then, into a rich family, no doubt, and will lose all interest in poor people like us. But why should he? You are willing to go to him for nothing. Why would anyone say no if he gets something for free? A bull steals into another man's garden not for any lack of feed, but because stolen grass tastes better. People wait long years for something they really want. Whichever way you look at it, it isn't good that you women keep going to Brindavan. Just think about it. Give it up."

That's what he said, and his wife replied: "I *have* thought about it. I even decided never to go back there. I hate this pretence. Do you remember that when I first heard the sound of his flute, I asked you two or three times if I should go, and you said yes. So I went. Would I have gone otherwise? But you were in no position to say no. Listen, man, I don't see any room here for liking or not liking."

God has put in his song a certain power that makes us lose ourselves. So let her go. Everything is a gift to God.

2

"All these women go to Brindavan
in the dead of night. What do they do there?
I have to find out."

He didn't have the guts to tell his wife
not to go, for fear she would leave him.
So he shaved off his mustache
and spent the day in the fields.
At night, he came home and dressed
himself in his wife's sari and blouse.
With his full chest, his hair tucked back
behind his ears, mascara around his eyes,
a dot on his forehead, and bangles (bought that morning)
on his arms, he rushed
to join the group of cowherd women
before it was too late. A little shy, he fit
right in. Soon a gentle sound

from the flute began, then swelled
to enfold them. He was looking
at the women. One held on to the sari
that was slipping from her waist.
Another tried to shrink her body so her
blouse would not burst open, and yet another
pressed her fingers to her lips, which felt bitten.
The hair of another woman was coming undone,
she turned her back and tried to fix it.

Not one of them was not
in agony. He stood there, alone,
like a plow-head removed from the plow.
Morning came. As if they had been making love
all night long, these women were propping up

their tired bodies, swaying like gentle streams
heavy with joy, rippling with smiles.
One straightened the necklace that was falling
from her neck. One touched up her hair,
all disheveled. One pulled her sari
back up to her waist. One loosened her blouse.
Caressed by the cool breeze of dawn,
they left, brushing against the rock

that was this man.

3

"Middle of the night! And in the forest? A stranger comes and plays
the flute and all of you, women of respectable families, dance for
him. This sort of wild behavior suits you and your village. Have your
men lost their manliness? That's your problem anyway. If a woman
in our town steps out of her doorway after dark, our men, tough as
tigers and venomous as cobras, cut her down with an ax by the
door. Is this some sort of a story or a play? I never knew such things
could happen in real life. In our family, it would never be allowed.
You say your husband doesn't mind. Why doesn't he? What kind of a
husband is he? And aren't you ashamed of having such a man for a
husband? If this were our town, what can I say, blood would flow.
Stop this."

When she finished her harangue, I left, laughing to myself.

I wanted to say, "He is a boy, he is God, no one loses her honor, and
our cowherds are hot-blooded, too." But she wouldn't listen. She is
too proud. She comes from a rich family and doesn't think much of
poor people.

I wanted to say, too, "If the goddess of wealth smiles on any one, it's
him." But I went away. She had a worm in her head.

Not a week passed, and I saw her in Brindavan, on a white moonlit night. I didn't talk to her. Why should I? She's the one who should be ashamed, not me. But she came to me and said, "I'm sorry for what I said. I didn't know that day. Don't hold it against me. If my people should come to know that I'm here, believe me, they'd kill me. Don't tell my parents, please. My father may kill me one day, but I didn't want to die without hearing this music."

4

She was laughing to herself.
Krishna pulled at her sari and asked what was going on.

—Krishna, I'm married. You shouldn't pull my sari.

—If you are another man's wife, why are you here with me in my forest? Did I ask you to come and joke with me? What if I did, did you have to accept? You could go tell your husband, couldn't you? The pleasure you get here is very discrete. If you want, I'll be your lover, and I'll take the blame. You have all the fun, and no one knows.

—Hey, there's no need to spell it out. Those who talk, talk about me. If any harm is done, it's to me. You won't lose a single feather from your peacock cap. Anyway, you asked me why I was laughing. I just had a thought. That crazy Surpanakha came to you in the forest; she wanted you, and she paid with her nose. It would have been so easy for her if she were a cowgirl now, in this village. That's why I laughed.

—I don't get it. Please explain.

—There's not much to say. Rama was a fair man.

—And I'm not? Is that what you think?

—Who am I to say that? But look: women don't have to want you very hard. They get your hugs without having to lose any noses or ears. Haven't you noticed?

She laughed again. Now there were two men standing in front of her, one rather stern.

5

You come while I'm taking my bath.
You come when my sari gets wet, and I change into a dry one.
When, unnoticed, my sari falls from my shoulder—you are there.
Almost as if you had planned it.
As if you knew all such slippery moments.
You sit right in front of me.

Some kids are like this from the start, in the womb.
You're a true jewel among them, the eye on a peacock's feather.
Really, you're spoiled. No one disciplines you.
Everyone loves you and no one speaks to you harshly.
Any time they begin to get mad,
you do something or other and they laugh,
and everything is lost in that laughter.
For years and years, your mother longed to have
a tiny boy in her womb, and you came, so now
she lets you do just as you please.

What's a game for the cat is death for the mouse.
We can't even talk about these things.
We can't face them unless we give up all shame.
Sometimes I tell myself firmly: he's only a child,
why get so stirred up? But that's how women are made.
I can't help myself. If *you*, young man,
are the one to take away my shame,
I will take you for my God.

When a woman is getting dressed, you should leave.
If you happen to catch a glimpse, you should
bite your tongue, go away, and come back after a while.
You should ask if you can come in.
That's the proper way. It's not as if
this is your own house and I'm your wife.
Even my husband doesn't come in when I'm dressing.

Along with being so brash, you're also angry.
Don't be.
Never mind what I said.
Come, Krishna, eyes dark
as the lotus.

Here Comes God

∾ TENNETI SURI

Hey, here comes God,
lifeless in bronze,
parading the streets,
riding his wooden horse.

Ask him about wages, fellows.
Tell him we don't have
enough to eat.

The wise men tell us
even stone hearts melt.
Let's see if that is true.

Bow down to him,
see if he listens,
and let go if he doesn't answer.

Hold up your hands
millions at once
raise your voice
so the sky itself shivers.

Ask him about the wages, fellows.
Tell him we don't have
enough to eat.

Seen from an Island in Godavari

~ ISMAIL

big white sheet of paper

a line across
and a line straight
on one corner

sailboat

what's below is river
and above is sky

could be

SURREALIST
DETOURS

When I lie down
my body curves and curls up
and asks me
"Who are you?"

Some People Laugh / Some People Cry

༄ SRI SRI

A man walks on the bridge and gives away the change in his pocket to a beggar. He gives away his wristwatch to a nurse who happens to walk towards him. He throws his coat into the river and follows the coat into the water.

A man knows all the ins and outs of this trade. Rupee trees sprout in his palm. They lay golden eggs in banks. Tears drip from them like yolk.

A man sits silently near a milestone. He waits as if someone may arrive any minute. He eats peas as he counts buses. He forgets all time looking at a cloud.

A man wanders about carrying ladders—he has goose eggs in his bag. He leans his ladder against a wall. He climbs the ladder and throws an egg up into the sky. He is the same guy who bought Harishchandra for a heap of gold that high.

A man investigates holes. They differ in size.

A man offers anarchy for sale. He appears to be wading in space, searching for something with his long arms. He eats nothing but the giant lemon found in the lakes of blood in the hearts of the young. That too, only once a day.

A man spends time singing Raga Kambhoji. It is not unnecessary to remind you that he has a lute with him. He has fingers only to legislate the ragas sung at appropriate times. At their touch stars catch fire. Lakes on the moon come to a boil. Winter begins to bud and my heart begins to offer marriage to the butterfly.

A man puts camphor in his eyes and red lead on his cheeks. He is a poet. He interprets the messages he receives in secret code and works for the air force. He is the one big reason for the fall of prices in the market.

A man meditates with a string of *rudraksha* beads around his neck. What's the use of your knowing that there's no use in my pleading with people not to break coconuts in front of him?

A man loves only one woman. She dies. Follow the rest of the story on the silver screen.

A man gets hanged. Society buys peace with his death. The law sighs with relief. Every evening a blind dog visits the spot where his blood was spilled and barks piteously. This man was so proud he refused to say he was unjustly hanged.

A man becomes great by making speeches. Another becomes poor by drinking too much. One takes a copper from his maternal aunt and buys a kite. Another grabs it from him.

A man runs away. Another fucks up his life. Another gets married. One man sleeps. Another dozes. Another talks and talks to while away time. One man's crying makes you laugh; another's laugh makes you cry. I can prove this with examples.

And on and on andonandonandonandon . . .

Sir, when will this end?
Son, this is endless.

The Sound of Silence

~ SRIRANGAM NARAYANA BABU

Cod-liver oil is rich in vitamin D.
Eggs improve your sperm count.
White birds are white, and black birds are black.
The sky is high, the earth is flat.
The Western Sky has beautiful red lips.
But how do you reach her?

When I lie down
my body curves and curls up
and asks me
"Who are you?"

The earth
turns emerald with grass all over,
scratches my foot and asks
"Who are you?"

A cool breeze pats my shoulder
morning and evening
and asks
"Who are you?"

Nature draws
two huge question marks
on the sky:

The Sound of Silence

"Who are you?"
"Who am I?"

I am the milk curdled in the breast
of the mother who died of thirst
after she delivered
on the Blue Hills.

I am that drop of undigested liquor
spilled from the stomach
during the autopsy
of the bastard who died
from drinking.

I am the breast milk
of that woman who delivered a dead child—
the woman who had to squeeze her milk
to relieve her pain—
in the dark of the night
into the gutter.

What does it matter who I am?
We met each other
when Rukmini was longing for love,
when we were thinking of family.

You and I
like the pound cake and the banana
that met each other on the cutting board.

However you count us
or, discount me
we are only two.

Blood is thicker than water.
Poets, brothers, bitter enemies—
whoever—
we are here:
Sri Sri and I.

When I dipped my pen in the inkwell
I hit a spider's web instead of ink.
There was a dead spider in it,
and two live flies.

I called Sri Sri
and asked "What's this brother?"

"The web is a lie.
That's a metaphor for poetic strategy.
The flies are you and I.
Krishna-Sastri fell in the inkwell and committed suicide,
'cause we didn't die in the web.
Our wings are broken
so let's crawl into the street."

I was finished with writing
but there was ink left.
"What do I do with it?" I asked.

"Leave it there. I will make
blue shawls with it
and give them as gifts to kings
who walk into my
revolutionary poems.

Or, drink it yourself,
until your blood turns blue.
Then light the lamp.

You are the red light to humanity.
You are the Plague-Police."

A big street yawned
and three girls were born.

It sneezed and
three street lamps lighted up.

I took a deep breath
and all of them disappeared.
Corpses of people who died from cholera
floated in the river of Time
like boats in Kashmir Lake.

"Streets are dangerous.
Let's run into the open, over there,"
said Sri Sri.

Both of us ran.
There was no wind there.
No light, no space.
The seven seas joined together
and were playing water-music.
The sky was lying in a corner
like a torn banana cup.
The snake Sesha lay dead
curling around the earth
like bathroom tissue.
Good and Bad
were flying like faded flags.

The root mountains
were going in the sky like aeroplanes.

Indra was rolling on the earth crying.
He lost his limbs to leprosy.
Saci, his wife, was feeling with her fingers
for any drops left over
in the empty pot of the juice of eternity.

Vajra
sat on Indra's throne,
gathered the mountain wings it had chopped,
and began to glue them back.

When the *ganda-bherunda* birds began to twitter
Sri Sri said, "Let's sing."

The goddess of poetry—
that washerwoman,
who had burned all the soiled words at the river—
appeared there, crying.
Sri Sri lifted his leg to kick her
and stood mute and motionless.

"What if they are lost?"
I said.

The volkslied the merchant of German words gave me when I
begged for it,
the *mutyala-saram*, that Gurajada bestowed on us,
the sprung rhythm borrowed from Hopkins—
all of them are lost,"
said Sri Sri, stammering.

How do we sing?
Sri Sri plucked a fang off the ancient snake
lying dead there
and drew a Dali picture on the female bird's wing.

The Sound of Silence

Here's a photograph of the picture
Man Ray-Narayna-Babu made.

The picture:

Two skeletons.
You do not look for beauty or sex in skeletons,
but one of them is a female skeleton
and the other is male.

The female skeleton holds a perfume bottle
and wears the brilliant Koh-i-noor diamond around her neck.
The male standing next to her
is crying, its bones have turned black from the heat.
It begins to dig up the Tajmahal
with a crowbar studded with diamonds.

Meanwhile, a female bird
picked up Sri Sri with its beak
and was carrying him off like an aeroplane.
I asked, "Where are you going?"
Sri Sri, who had no words,
made a sign with his hand:
"To the Land of the Eagles."

I began to forget language.
I kept repeating my words
so I wouldn't lose them all.

Meanwhile,
Time was groaning, hitting the walls
cemented with the dreams of humanity—
all the dreams it had dreamed since the first night.
I sat for a while
stretching my feet into the end of Time.

Boundaries were getting mixed up.
The walls of space were breaking.
I got up.
When I saw the Silver Mountain
I climbed onto it.

A flower garden in a valley.
All flowers, no trees.
Upanishads were singing like bees.
Parvati stood naked, plucking flowers.
Shiva was sleeping.
When I saw Parvati,
I ejaculated in my pants.

I was on fire.
I stood mute.
There appeared a silent conch nearby.
I touched the silent conch.
It cried: *so'ham*, I am Him.

My consciousness turned into the foam
on the seven seas and evaporated on their trillion arms.
The Moon rose in my bone marrow.
My body became the ashes of the first father
and my life-breath became the tireless sage who
brought the heavenly river from the sky.
The river rained on my spine,
and Parvati patted my soft belly with her cool, icy hands.

Sound is another name for silence.

Myth of Myself

∽ SRI SRI

What can he do poor man?
Wave after wave
trouble after trouble
like red pepper on an open wound
and a pestle blow on top of it.

What can he do?
How many things can he cry over?
Indira Gandhi's son died.
A Naxalite killed a police officer.
Somewhere some time ago someone
tore up his jack of spades.
How long can he cry over these things?

Kodavatiganti died of a heart attack.
The sun is getting colder day by day
without telling anybody at all.
Language does not have the breath
to keep pace with the speed
of thought.
How long can he cry over these things?

Therefore in that grief
he entered a pumpkin.
A housewife bought it and
cut it in two right down the middle.
He sensed the danger even as the housewife
picked up her kitchen knife,

skillfully reduced his size and
hid himself in the stem of the pumpkin.

The housewife threw the stem on the garbage heap.
A cow swallowed it.
Do cows eat pumpkin stems?
Don't doubt it.
If she's hungry, a cow can eat
all the newspapers in Andhra.

Well, he's moving about freely
in the intestines of the cow.
He changed his body into chemicals.
Aha! Moving about in the belly of the cow
is like staying in a five-star hotel.

Suddenly he asked himself "Why am I here?
I must go back to my world."
He returned through the cow's shit and pizzle.
He's now back among men.
He turned the chemicals back into his own shape.

He entered the Bay of Bengal and took a bath.
All the dirt's washed off.
He stood straight,
waved his hands in the air,
and got the clothes he needed
(a medieval baba trick).

Challenging the world, he said:
"I'm not going to surrender
to the hardships you give me."

Who is he?
No other than Sri Sri.

TROUBLED
WORDS

*Sentences do not deliver
what you wanted them to say.*

Really?

~ SRI SRI

Really?
Will all the world find happiness?
People see good times?
Really?

Really?
Does the world laugh
happily forever?
Does it overcome
its desire to kill?

Does the time when chains
tighten on slaves
end forever?
Do friendship and brotherhood,
their gentle ways,
win the day?

The dance of the oceans
with their hair disheveled
and waves curled up—
will it end at last?
The boat that's caught
in the middle of the storm—
will it safely reach the shore?
Really?
Really?

Death of Man

~ ARUDRA

Sentences do not deliver
what you wanted them to say.
Like a gramophone record stuck in a track,
words repeated over and over, on and on,
say nothing.
Education refuses to perform acrobatics
on the rope of government jobs
in the circus that is this world.
Knowledge ceases to tick like a clock
in the magnetic field of power.
Science does not resolve problems.
Mathematics refuses to increase food production.
Freedom ceases to flourish
in the dreary land of red tape.
The chutney is not done by the court time
in the law clerk's kitchen blender.
The grocer refuses to give groceries
on credit.
Man, may you live long,
this is the prelude.

The fear that ran through
the mind of primitive man
is running through yours.
The dark forces of his brain,
his hand,
his cry,

delude you.
You can't see the visible.
You can't grasp the baseless.
You can't recognize the past.
You can't recognize your present.
Your eye is a five-year-old child.

Sentences add a mustache and a beard
to the female faces of intended thoughts.
Guns openly ridicule men.
In the circus that is this world
dictators chew up
people's lives.
Science creates insoluble problems
in huge numbers, day after day.

Mathematics skips
the school of human needs.
Education goes on sick leave without salary.
Knowledge swallows a cyanide capsule.
The *Kamasutra* is taught in college bathrooms.
The law clerk demands double his bribe.
Prices of groceries multiply themselves.
Man, may you live long,
this is the end.

The desire frozen in the libido
of primitive man
is melting in you.
The hunger in his eyes
embraces you,
his scream
amazes you.
You can't see what's really happening.
You can't name things that have no name.

Death of Man

You can't change today's date
nor can you recognize your present.
Your unconscious
is like the rain forest
on the first day of creation.

Meaning that should be contained in a word
usurps sentence after sentence.
Card games try to hatch the egg of the future.
Horses grow fat on the wages of laborers.
Every sword thrown in the big circus that is this world
hits the breasts of your girlfriend
hidden in the box.
Special expeditions of mountaineers set off to scale
the salaries of movie stars
instead of Mount Everest.
Desires that retired
apply again to the jobs advertised.
Students' allowances
flow to the red-light district.
Red tape continues to rule unfettered
while the red flag hides behind the western hills
to prepare for a revolution.
Labor leaders' skulls are found
when land is plowed.

After a dozen shots of whisky
informed circles recognize danger.
The state department
ducks all questions from the press
and begins to discuss the problem.
Representatives from big business
successfully negotiate
relief from additional taxes
on rumor mills.

Governments nationalize the sale of lies.
The law clerk's wife gives birth to his seventh daughter.
Groceries disappear into the black market.
It's curtains for normal life.
Man, may you live long,
this is hell.

The hidden key
revealed to primitive man
in his hunger
is offered to you as a boon.
Your awareness
is fully ripe.

Man, may you live long,
you are me.

Who Is Awake in the Dead of Night?

∽ BAIRAGI

Who is awake in the dead of night?
Who knows that lamps deceive,
shadows conspire,
and darkness has a feeble mind?
Who knows?

In that room silent as a grave,
what good is that streak of light?

A tangle of sad thoughts pacing the floor
and a trapped bird,
like a blade of grass that cannot fly.

Who understands?
Tomorrow is another day. Nothing more to say.

The vigil, a leaky boat in the ocean of dark,
the pain of climbing the mountain of dawn that has no steps,
a pathway of faint light to find your way through dark,
a constant thought that someone's at the door,
timid thoughts that run like rats through the mind's empty house,
barking dogs, holes in the blanket.

Who understands them,
if not the one who is awake?

Midnight has no friends,
no company for the sleepless.

Many are here,
but they are all sleeping,
lucky people,
they've no worries.
For them the long endless night is a sweet moment of rest,
this dark hard road is a bed of black lilies.
A leisurely walk on a soft path shaded by satin eyelids.
Their world is on the other side of the river of death.

But what keeps the sleepless man awake?
What steals the cash of sleep from his eyelid wallet?
Humiliation, pride, thorny memories?
Dark turns of a shameful life?
Or why should anyone be awake now,
when the whole world sleeps?

"*When it is night for everyone*
the sage stays awake."
Who doesn't wish for a boat ride of dreams
in the dark lake of sleep,
the sway of steady breathing on the soft lap of waves?

But someone should be awake here.
When he who hasn't come shows up, unexpected,
who'll open the door for him, who'll say hello?
When the petals of the morning flower open,
who raises the broken throat of peace?
When the last soldier of the night's defeated army
comes home wounded,
when the first messenger from the front line,
crosses over the falling bridge of flesh and bones,
and brings future thoughts,
who'll talk to him, who'll know him?
Who is awake all night?

The Vedantist

∿ SRI SRI

You say it's nothing,
it's all an illusion.

My friend, Vedantist,
what do you say?

What we see isn't there?
What we hear isn't real?
The world doesn't exist?
A dream
unreal
nothing, nothing?

You say it's nothing?

The Rolls Royce of the rich man
is nothing?

The thick wallet of the millionaire
is nothing?

The machine gun, the poison gas
are nothing?

You say they're nothing?

The farmer's sweat
the worker's grief
the beggar's hunger

they are nothing?

Hurricanes, earthquakes,
revolts, war
war war war war.

All nothing?
Nothing?

What do you say? Nothing?

The world's not real
it's a dream
an illusion
nothing, nothing.
Really?

You say it's all nothing?

Memories

〜 SISHTLA UMA-MAHESWARA RAO

My name is Lila.
I came, came here to get out of that town. That handsome
young man did me in. I am far away from every one
and think of all of them. Women of the neighborhood stop by,
ask silent questions with their piercing eyes and go away.
Sleepless and alone in the middle of night, I long for death.

I remember grandmother, mother, my little sister and father.
I remember my brothers, the younger and the older but
you are my real memory.
Why don't you come?
It's night, my sweet man,
my love is real.

I think of you at dawn.
I think of me think of you.
I think of you when I am in bed.
Come as my pillow,
hold me tight.

I remember you in winter.
I remember you in spring.
I remember you in rain.

I remember you when you don't answer.
Come, my man, tall and handsome.

I remember you answering
as I call you alone from a far away place.

I remember whatever I do
all alone.

Your memories dig deep in my thoughts.

Did you seduce another girl?
Did you trap another woman?
Come soon, come now.
I am getting attracted
to other men here.

I long for a child.
Married women
can have a child.
Only married women
can rock the cradle.

Rock a by baby ... on the tree top ...

Who caused your birth, my little child?
Whoever it is, he is not a man.

Rock a by baby ...

Are you a boy? Are you a girl?
If you are a boy you will not
ruin women's lives.
If you are a girl, you will not
ruin your life for men.

Because,
the virgin goddess delivered you,

the goddess of death fed you milk,
the goddess' brother gave you a bath.

Rock a by baby on the tree top . . .

Where is my baby, where has it gone?
Who took my baby, who took it away?

My breasts are full, the cradle is empty.
Milk in my breasts is curdled hard,
I turn into a rock,
a hard rock.

God, Rama,
My name is Lila.

Dateline Hyderabad

1990 December 8

∽ AJANTA

At midnight, when all the Lords of the Directions are resting, a man sits by
his own corpse on a side street in the city and says:

"I didn't die.
Who are you?
Why are you taking me away in your vehicle?
No. Don't, don't touch me.
This is my body."

The man continues, stroking his smooth dead body:

"I work hard for a living.
I live here.
They kicked me in the dark right here.
Pierced me with knives.
They cut my hands and feet.
They don't know who I am; I don't
know who they are."

He holds both my hands and asks piteously:

"Will you lend me half of your body?
I want to live just one more time.
Or will you lend me your hands and feet?
I will go search for my wife and children."

"Don't you want eyes, too?"

"No, I don't. I don't want to see blood.
Hands and feet will be my eyes."

I give him all he wants to use forever.
The next minute he's not there.
He disappears into the lake of darkness,
carrying his own dead body.
I stay there holding my eyes
unable to bear them
unable to die.

*"All people are one; all gods are one," a demonic voice fiercely sobs in the
middle of the street. The earth explodes and smoke spreads across the sky.*

Sleep

∽ AJANTA

nobody nowhere they've all gone home
the student has closed his books
the street singer stopped his song
nobody nowhere—they've all gone home

murderers have put away their knives
demons have gone to the underworld
statesmen have washed the blood off their hands
nobody nowhere—they've all gone home

they all looked at their faces in the mirror
saw what was there in that abyss
they shut the doors before death opened its mouth
nobody nowhere—they've all gone home

workers dried their tears in their huts under the moonlight
prisoners flew between bars into the sky
beggars covered themselves with posters on the sidewalk
nobody nowhere—they've all gone home

whores took off their poisoned clothes
carefully hung their tear-drenched breasts on the wall
nobody nowhere—all are asleep
they've hidden the rest of their life in the basement

demons, politicians, ministers, heads of state
common folk, gentlemen—all are asleep

Sleep

they all took cover in the shelter of night
flags do not fly now
clocks do not move
nobody nowhere—all are asleep
all took cover in the shelter of night
there is no difference now between the killer and the killed
the ugly and the beautiful look alike now
there is no barbed wire between man and man
no one is aware of the fear of death
nobody nowhere—all are asleep
they've all taken cover in the shelter of night

deadly snakes shed their skin now
unseen worlds breathe outside time
nobody nowhere—all are asleep
they've all taken cover in the shelter of night

no thoughts chase like wolves this night
tiger-life does not scare anyone now
nobody nowhere—all are asleep
they've all taken cover in the shelter of night

you won't hear the sound of guns until tomorrow
men who've surrounded the globe do not fight in the dark
you won't hear recorded war music anywhere now
nobody nowhere—all are asleep
they've all taken cover in the shelter of night

no fear of postmen, not until tomorrow
the letter the murderer mailed will not be delivered yet
no mother grieves for sons who left home
no one knows yet if friend turned against friend
nobody nowhere—all are asleep
they've all taken cover in the shelter of night

no expectations, jealousies, no despair
no long sighs, hatred, horrors
no hardships, no tears
one silence all over
one heartbeat

Me on the Wall

∽ AJANTA

The mirror is not your body hanging from the wall
It's you

There's always a magician behind your image
And a hero on a horse
A clown breaking into the secrets of the world outside

The mirror is your innermost world

Since I couldn't bring out
the images moving on waves in the mirror
I entered straight into the mirror myself
Now what's in the mirror is not my image

It's me
without a body

Give Me Confidence

∽ BAIRAGI

Give me confidence
I'll pulverize the mountains,
shove the sun and moon from the sky
like a mushy tomato or a broken cracker
from a dirty dinner plate.

I'll roll up this vast universe
like a mat in my strong arms.

I'll erase man's unlucky fate
off his forehead,
banish injustice from the assembly of life
and kick
all aggression out.

I'll do more, much more.
But give me confidence.

I'll fight the god of death.
I'll stand upside down on the trident of Shiva.
I'll make daydreams blossom in every house
and make them yield fruit—
six for three.

Like the comedian
with a wooden gun,

Give Me Confidence

I'll have wells leveled and
tanks dug.

If the world is too crowded for people,
I'll have a hospice built
in another world.

I'll cut cloth from the purple sky
and have shirts made for everyone.

I can do anything.
But give me confidence.

Confidence.

Hades

∾ VEGUNTA MOHANA PRASAD

hey boatman
come
my eyes can't see and it's slippery
dark here
this breeze blows off my shawl
it's cold, cold my throat's frozen
flowers here smell
like fire
like my eyes
the light runs through my nerves
I call out for you
the sky is drowned
marble floats up
the burning fire crackles
clears my throat
hey you, come here
one handful of moon can't quench this fire
flowers all over the woods
fire all over the forest
smoke all over the river
how can the boat come
hey come here come here
closer closer to this shore

Empty

∾ VEGUNTA MOHANA PRASAD

Over
They all left
Each their own way
An absent-minded umbrella
Sandals that can't spell
Paper wrappers with no cakes
The whole floor, an ashtray
Nothing remains
Nothing happens, ever
Except for the December flowers that fall
after the sun goes behind the hill
Except for the ants at the bottom
of the teacup empty of life
Emptiness
after the feast
You have to spread it
a little here, a little there
You have to fold the chairs
shake the tablecloth
count the cups
put a foot over the wrist watch someone dropped
sip a little of the leftover coffee
shed a tear or two
You have to straighten emptiness
a little here and a little there

How mercilessly guests go!

Stupidity

∾ VEGUNTA MOHANA PRASAD

If they let me go into the temple
—why only my shirt—
I would have taken all my clothes off

Anyway
the fellow outside offered to take
my picture just as I am

If I waited a little longer
I would be a saint
rubbing my eyes in the red of the evening
watching one sky and
three oceans

Luckily
I was hungry
and thirsty too
in the bar

All night
three full skies slept in me
When I woke up at last
they turned into one ocean of
grief
a blood dot sprang in the east
on my hapless face

Chasing Memory

〜 TRIPURANENI SRINIVAS

Always a nagging feeling, that I forgot something. When I look back,
a transparent shadow chases me. It doesn't look like me. That's why
I suspect it. Something I lost calls me from behind the curtains.
When I peep inside, I see a heart half slashed still beating. It doesn't
sound like me. That's the problem. Well, maybe I shouldn't have
any doubts. I am probably there behind the drooping sky, all alone.
My memory might still be shining in the emptiness behind the sky.
I don't deny it. Neither do I accept it. But the memory follows me.
I keep searching thoughtfully for the lamp that fell off the shores of
forgetfulness. I crawl on the hands of the clock and I feel the pieces
of cloud that fell a time ago. That's what everyone does. No one
remembers what they forgot. They can't reach out and touch what
they lost. That's how everybody is. Ask the wild plant that grows like
an axe on the wall; it will tell you. Even the sun's little finger that
falls on the window and peeps cautiously into the room will tell
you. We forgot something. We lost something. When we think of
that, our heart gets wet with memory. An ocean crosses the shore
under the eyelids, wave after wave. A single teardrop weeps alone on
the cheek. Flowers fall dead in the garden of memories. They remind
you again and again you forgot what you forgot. Smile? It's always
there. Pain? It's there too. It's only the dumb memory that can not
talk. You can ask the dew that walked on the sunny path. You can
measure for a change the distance that multiplies itself between
people. You can also call the secret light that hangs in the empty
space behind the clouds. Never mind, the memory that should
remind you of what you forgot only reminds you that you forgot.
Never mind, it breaks your limbs into pieces and flies each in a

different sky as a delicate kite. At least we have the memory. We'll go forward holding on to this. To find out what we lost, to remember what we forgot, to reach out for the touch we lost. Just don't let go of the finger and don't stop walking. You should always remember you forgot something.

VOICES OF REVOLUTION

We write: Long Live Revolution!

The Wheels of Jagannatha

~ SRI SRI

you are downtrodden
ruined
bitten by pain
you are burnt
wasted
crushed under the chariot of evil

humble
low
you have nothing to eat
no place to live
you are poor

friends have deserted you
people have rejected you
society has cast you out
you have lost hope
no goal to reach
no home to go to
but don't cry
don't

the wheels are coming
the wheels of Jagannatha
the Juggernaut of justice
the wheels
the wheels

The Wheels of Jagannatha

are coming
are coming

you who are fallen
you who are broken
the wheels
from the sky
they are coming
they are coming

they're crushing the mountains
the Himalayas
the Vindhyas
all the great mountains
they're all crushed
they're crushed
they're broken
the Juggernaut is moving

you who are fallen
you who are broken
you are welcome here

homeless you live
outside the town
under the tree
with your pots and pans
your everything in a bag
darkness everywhere
prison
gallows
suicide
death
brothers, you are deceived
I know your problems

your suffering
your story
I understand

you who are fallen
you who are down
you who are deceived

here I come
I will wield my pen
for you for you
I will bring the wheels to earth
the wheels of Jagannatha
the speeding rushing wheels
the roaring running wheels
I will turn them toward the earth
I will make the earth quake

the third eye of Shiva
has opened fire
it will burn the world
the fire in the eye
the furious eye
kill kill
this is war
this is the end
one way or the other
the day is ours
you who are fallen
you who are down
this is final
this is the end

this is war
this iron eagle

The Wheels of Jagannatha

this feast of fire
will end injustice
will kill the evil

Freedom
Fraternity
Equality
Love
will make a new world
peace peace
the dream is true
this heaven is real

brothers who are fallen
brothers who are down
cry no more
the wheels are here
the wheels are close
the wheels of justice
the wheels of power
are here my brothers
come here my brothers
this world is yours
rule this kingdom

We Should Remember

∾ KALOJI

They ruined our lives.
They raped our women.
They killed our children.
They imprisoned us—

those despicable creatures,
the demons in power.

We should mark them well
with burning anger
and hit them hard
when the time comes.

"Peace and nonviolence" should not deter us.
"Pity and compassion" should not delay us.
Make no peace if they talk peace.
We should not forgive if they beg for life.

We should wait for the time,
play all the tricks,
but hit them we must
when the time comes.

Cut the tongue that lashed out at us,
burn the hands that groped our women,
blind the eyes that coveted our girls,

We Should Remember

break the legs that kicked us.
Piece by piece,
feed those bastards to the crows.

Hit them hard
when the time comes.

Warrior, Bhaskar!

~ SIVUDU

Under the *narrenga* tree, Warrior, Bhaskar
You were furious, your eyes red, Warrior, Bhaskar
You were furious, your eyes red, Warrior, Bhaskar
You leapt to fight, Warrior, Bhaskar

Under the *barrenka* tree, Warrior, Bhaskar
You picked up your gun, Warrior, Bhaskar
Picked up your gun, Warrior, Bhaskar
and broke the chains, Warrior, Bhaskar

Under the *gottanki* tree, Warrior, Bhaskar
You sharpened your axe, Warrior, Bhaskar
You sharpened your axe, Warrior, Bhaskar
You killed the enemy, Warrior, Bhaskar

Under the *vippa* tree, Warrior, Bhaskar
You strung your bow, Warrior, Bhaskar
You strung your bow, Warrior, Bhaskar
You yelled "We won," Warrior, Bhaskar

They saw your courage, Warrior, Bhaskar
They were scared and mad, Warrior, Bhaskar
Scared and mad, Warrior, Bhaskar
They cut off your head, Warrior, Bhaskar

Under the *singeri* tree, Warrior, Bhaskar
They cut off your head, Warrior, Bhaskar

Warrior, Bhaskar!

They cut off your head, Warrior, Bhaskar
They jumped with joy, Warrior, Bhaskar

The blood that gushed out, Warrior, Bhaskar
They poured it into bottles, Warrior, Bhaskar
"What's in the bottles?" Warrior, Bhaskar
They said, "It's wine," Warrior, Bhaskar

The blood that spilled, Warrior, Bhaskar
They put it in pots, Warrior, Bhaskar
"What's in the pots?" Warrior, Bhaskar
They said, "It's toddy," Warrior, Bhaskar

The blood that dripped, Warrior, Bhaskar
They poured into pans, Warrior, Bhaskar
"What's in the pans?" Warrior, Bhaskar
They said, "It's milk," Warrior, Bhaskar

The blood that clotted, Warrior, Bhaskar
They put it in cups, Warrior, Bhaskar
"What's in the cups?" Warrior, Bhaskar
They said, "It's curds," Warrior, Bhaskar

To kill you, to kill us, Warrior, Bhaskar
To hide and to bite, Warrior, Bhaskar
To bite with their venom, Warrior, Bhaskar
They plotted and planned, Warrior, Bhaskar

The path you took, Warrior, Bhaskar
Is the path of heroes, Warrior, Bhaskar
The path you took, Warrior, Bhaskar
We will take up the gun, Warrior, Bhaskar

Under the *barrenka* tree, Warrior, Bhaskar
We took up the gun, Warrior, Bhaskar
Took up the gun, Warrior, Bhaskar
We broke our chains, Warrior, Bhaskar

We Write

∾ SIVA REDDY

Don't know whose house don't know
who lives there
but we write: Long Live Revolution!

Don't know if that's a shop or a jail
Don't know if that's a compound wall or a parliament hall
but we write: Long Live Revolution!
Right across the road, in between two lampposts
we write: Long Live Revolution!
We write on Nehru's forehead at the intersection: Long Live
    Revolution!

On crowded buses
on trains and cars smooth like bald heads
on schools, colleges
on the nerve centers of universities
we write: Long Live Revolution!

On water
on rivers that carry water
on canals running like fingers of rivers, on rice fields
on crops, on the soil of the crops
on the labor of hands living off the earth
on paths, on bushes among paths
on foot paths leading into villages
on the handfuls of dust in the paths
we write: Long Live Revolution!

On hills
on the wide-chested sky, standing on the heads of hills
on clouds that are the thoughts of the sky
on rain
on every drop of rain
on the new light descending with every drop
on seeds that capture the light
on the sea of rice seedlings
we write: Long Live Revolution!

On pieces of scrap paper torn and thrown out
on every letter glowing on those pieces of paper
on little tiny lights
on peace slogans
on every sound born in every palate
we write: Long Live Revolution!

We write on leaves
on the forest
on the trees
on the bark
on the leaf buds breaking out of the trees
on every finger, on every leg
on every foot and on every footprint
on every breath
on the blood of every boy growing up brilliantly
on every sun rising out of that blood
we write: Long Live Revolution!

We write: Long Live Revolution!

Live Walls

∾ MAHE JABEEN

The night that orders everyone to sleep
stays awake for us
Our work sings the morning song

We don't even remember the warmth of our youth
We embrace walls in the dark
We touch them with messages for revolution
We decorate them red
Walls grow young

The red words from the white walls
provoke us

We walk looking for more white walls
yet untouched
We lose ourselves in the color of beauty
for a minute
Then we become aware
and stand before the walls fully awake
We capture every wall we can find
and we passionately embrace it
to kiss what we wrote on it
Police batons kiss us instead

With our blood as witness
every wall speaks
our words

WORDS
OF DESPAIR,
SONGS OF HOPE

*I
even I
added
a piece of wood
to the fire of the world*

The Night It Rained Life

🙚 DEVARAKONDA BALAGANGADHARA TILAK

The night it rained life
you were all sleeping

I opened the door
left home
and walked
beyond the hill
beyond the valley
into the open
and I stood there
in the moonlight

Gods' women
danced in the sky
the stars, their anklets, chimed in rhythm
bunches of flowers hung from their hair
young in the curves of their breasts
they moved like stringed bows
they played and laughed
and said:

Look here
a handsome man
happiness in his heart
silken tassels of dreams on his crown
a song in the sparkle of his eyes
a lyric of smiles on his lips

The Night It Rained Life

He knows secrets no one knows
he loves life, knows life
he's the sun who rises on the ocean of our dreams
he is our lover, our husband
the man

Lasting life showered on me
the fullness of youth flowed in streams
I drank it with both my hands
I said goodbye to death and grief
wore a shawl of sweet desire
and life as a garland of smiling flowers
I set foot on the path of victory

The night it rained life
you were all sleeping
tired from your day you embraced habit
you slept enslaved for fear of the new
you didn't hear the call to the Festival of Joy

That's why you do not know
I live

An Announcement

~ SRI SRI

I
even I
added
a piece of wood
to the fire of the world

Even I
gave a tear of mine
to the rain of the world

I offered my voice too
to the roar of the world

In summer's hot sun
I burned like a bird

In the monsoon rains
I was wet to the skin

In winter I suffered
stiff
in hunger and cold

If I alone cease
hot wind, rain, and snow
are wasted on this earth

An Announcement

The colorful stars
that look from the sky
fall to the earth
vomiting blood

Days will explode
Nights get shattered
The world will end
in a catastrophe

A day will come
when I pervade the world
when my song of the dark night
thrills the earth

I will open
like the white petal
of the world lotus

I will sing
like the string of the
world lyre

I will fly
like the flag on the
top of the world

A Blade of Grass

◌ SRIRANGAM NARAYANA BABU

Go ahead,
walk over me
I am only a blade of grass.

When you worship,
I am your flower,
the *durvankura* you offer to your gods.
When you are finished,
I am grass.
Go ahead,
walk on me!

You ride on palanquins,
walk on carpets.
I am soft as silk.
Walk on me!

Your cows love me.
I adorn your feet.
I am a blade of grass.
Walk on me.

The smallest speck of dust
on your tender feet
hurts my heart
like a meteor shower.

A Blade of Grass

Walk over me,
I will take care of you.

You know my brother
that sharp fellow.
He split the tongues of snakes
right down the middle.

We decorate your finger
when you feed your fathers.
They pass to heaven
over our bodies.

The red of the sky
says the earth is strong.
The west wind at dawn
tells me my story.

Yes, I am the one who punished the demon.

Now I know.
Stop.
You can't walk over me.

A Prayer

⌘ DEVARAKONDA BALAGANGADHARA TILAK

God
save this country
from saintly men, chaste women
from those who preach morals with both their tongues
from snakes who hiss pure compassion
from millions of deities, their priests, their agents
from theorists, theologians, and the long lineage of teachers
all the way down to my own.

God
this is a country of four hundred million
people who are truly living.
This is a strange land of hunger and pain
struggle and suffering
food for the belly, love for the heart
freedom to live
a little good
and a little bad
a few tears and a cup of smiles—
God
that's all we want.

We want to live honestly
have fun, have pity
no pretenses, nothing to boast of
no fences around us, no easy answers.

A Prayer

God
let us hear the song
stopped in the throat
that was severed by the sword.
Help us read the pages of our history
soiled by our own blood.

Show us that brilliant waterfall of light—
your mysterious creation.

Be kind to us.

Life is an uncertain pause between birth and death
and it's dark all around.
The only solace is we're still human
smelling like sandalwood.

We tire at every step
fall at every turn.
Let us rest for a while
on a bed of hopes,
on flowers of our dreams.

Father
permit us to forget our pain
for just a little while.

A Bitter Poem

∽ SRI SRI

it's true
what you said is true
it's true

no happiness
in this world
life's a waste
education
poetry
all are a waste

we are slaves
wheels in machines
we are deceived
left and right
all around

this is no life
worse than dogs
pigs in alleys

you are right
you are right
life's a shadow
learning's a fraud
poetry is a bitter fruit

A Bitter Poem

no pleasure
no taste
the fruit of life is
utterly bitter

it's true
it's true
what you said is true

This Night

∾ REVATI DEVI

If this night passes
if this night, which does not surrender even to sleeping pills
passes

the night that spreads under my back
like a bed of arrows
for not compromising with man

the night that flows in my veins
like blood from the thorns of the toddy palm
for not compromising with God
if this night passes

day covers the face of honesty
with a blanket of light
another day another night another day

what if sometime another night another day
honesty stands naked, smooth
not finding light
if that night stands without passing
I will pass, I will move away, honestly

No Break

∽ REVATI DEVI

midnight
no sound no light no breeze
darkness in sleep middle of night
midnight in sleep midsleep in night
from somewhere of someone
a child's cry tearing out of its mother's womb
the last look of a person drained of life
cry for help of an animal caught by a tiger
sparkle of a murderer's knife
the first imprint of lovers' lips
sound of the night-watchman's stick
heartbeat of fear
whore's eyes searching for a customer in the shadows of the lamppost
the helpless face of a person hanging herself
unresolved questions in an intellectual's mind
burning stomach of a person who ate days ago
ticking of the clock on the table
train's whistle dashing through the cold on the bridge
from somewhere of someone

Wooden Horse

∽ NAGNAMUNI

It's a lie
to say life's an illusion.
Only crows perched on electric wires,
on rooftops,
eating scraps of food from garbage,
poking at carcasses
and the wounds of helpless people—
only crows
preach illusion,
caw sermons.

It's a lie to say humanity is alive.
Only tigers looking for lamb's skins
lecture on morals in public.

Poetry is a lie.
Poetry that says
It is for the good of the world
and gets stuck between the thighs of young heroines
in erotic poems
and in the stories of ointments you rub on your feet
to make yourself fly.

It's not to the mountains
you should go for austerities.
Go to the people.

Wooden Horse

It's not your family you renounce,
it's your self.

What lasts in all languages
as the ultimate sound
isn't OM
but the cry for help.

It's a lie to say technology opens the path of truth.
It's a lie to say that man grows civilized as centuries pass.
The last breath of man
endlessly groaning for life,
rolling on the sidewalk
is real.
Death is real.

The silent corpse is real.
Poverty's real.
The darkness poverty spreads is real.
The blood in the veins of the worker
who creates wealth—
that's real.

Life's a plowshare.
It plows the skin and fills it with furrows.
The crop of experience
yields gold.
But the farmer's left with
a cactus in his mouth
and tears in his eyes.

The rocket soars toward the moon
while a mosquito settles on it
and sings the song of space,
ridiculing the progress of science.

2

Poetry is the gravedigger
who buries syllables in paper.

Every syllable that emerges from the poet
kills the idea in its womb
and makes the poet a murderer.

The true poet suspects
every syllable he uses.

Every limb of man
tries to change into an animal
throughout its life.

All the planets in the cosmos
go round and round
to influence the earth.

What's left at the end
is murder.
No wound.
No blood.

3

I am probably singing
only one song.
I will sing it all my life.
I will pull a gut from my stomach,
make it a one-stringed lute
and play it
from street to street.

Wooden Horse

I will keep searching
for the ear
that can hear the truth.

4

In every farmer
who goes to his farm
with a plow on his shoulder,
his skinny bullocks following him
early in the morning
before sunrise,
I see Jesus carrying his cross.

Yes,
I'm talking about murder.

Jesus knows who betrays him
at the last supper.
I know who the murderers are.
But for the time being,
I blame it on the ocean.

The calendar doesn't have a body.
It's a bone in the mouth of dog-time.
It's a piece of paper stuck on the wall
like a gecko.
Dates stand dumb
like the accused on the stand.
It could be any day,
November 19th
for instance.

No signs of tears on the calendar
except disasters and jokes.

Weeks lie down like patients
with a blanket over them.
White paper paints over the pain hidden under the blanket.
White blood oozes when time is cut into weeks and days.
If you lift the blanket and hear the pain behind the white blood,
it could be any day, any week.
But the eye of time was stuck to the hook of Saturday
and it froze kicking.

In nature or in culture,
the only truth is the demonic darkness
that rules over men.

Humanity
is the ray of light
born and dead
every day, every minute.

5

The peace conference meets in Geneva.
Worship is offered in temples.
Free food is given in soup kitchens.
Prayers are held in mosques.
The devils chant scriptures
in many voices, in all languages.

The freed dove goes right into the cat's mouth.
Hunger holds its sides and laughs
at free food and prayer.

One who has food knows
how to control hunger when it rebels.
The finger on the trigger knows
whose heart the bullet shoots through.

I know who the murderers are.
As a poet, as a pretender,
I blame Time
for the time being.

Fully dressed,
civilization escapes into nudity.
It tries to lose itself in the eyes
of the dancers in the cabaret.
But hunger is there too.
Hunger in infinite forms
haunting man all his life.
Rat holes are all over life.
People don't live, they escape.
The whole world is running
from an unknown reality, whatever it is.
Running, gasping for breath,
as if death were chasing it,
sword in hand.

You don't need a sword
to cut off people's life breath.
You don't need guns and battles
to destroy people,
to turn them into corpses
instantly.
Water's enough.
Water can quench your thirst and keep you alive.
It can also kill.

Be it human cruelty,
or natural disaster
it's the bones of the poor that break.
What's left at the end are dead huts.
You can see them from a helicopter,

from an airplane.
Or take a peek at them
hiding inside your car,
under the cover of your cap,
behind newspaper statements.
Or see them close up, shake them.
Or see them in compassion, love,
in a helping gesture,
hiding your hypocrisy, cruelty.
However you see,
you see only one picture:
Waves of silent grief.
But never mind.
A corpse doesn't ask for an explanation.

Jesus knows
who deceives him at the last supper.
I know who the murderers are.
But for a while,
I blame it on Nature.

Once,
there was a village here.
Once the land and the air and the sky here
were filled with people.
You could see and hear their songs,
laughter, sorrows, sighs, words of comfort.
Leaves swam green in the air.
Rows of birds mischievously
pecked at fruit
and chirped notes of love in hushed tones.

Once
crops heavy with golden grain
danced here in graceful waves.

Wooden Horse

Shame on Time.
Shame on History.
Shame on Creation.

The weak man creates wealth.
The strong man devours wealth and distributes poverty.
History is littered with the corpses of the poor.

6

The horse
that carried the future Buddha
in the middle of the night
to the end of the empire
when he left his palace,
his wife,
his son,
his parents
and all his wealth and kingdom—
the horse still stands
in tears
on Nagarjuna Hill.
But the tree of wisdom
died in man's mind
long ago.

7

The horse
is a sign of speed and faith,
victory and strength of rule.
The wooden horse,
a symbol of stagnation
stupidity
ignorance

egoism
and inefficient government.
The heart of the horse
stands still, in tears.
The wooden horse, however,
neighs
like a counterfeit coin.
The wooden horse doesn't walk the earth.
It rides the shoulders of the poor
with iron hooves and a plastic heart,
proud of its money.

If you lift your head
under its weight
it neighs furiously
and crushes you.

Governments ride
the wooden horse and wield
a wooden sword
like the obscene images
on temple walls.

8

Jesus knows
who betrays him at the last supper.

I know there are huts along the coast.
There are anthills near the huts.
There are cobras in the anthills.
There is poison in those fangs.
I know that the cobra hoods of the waves wait
to bite the hand that feeds them milk.
I know who the murderers are.

But I blame it on the ocean
for now.

Dreams bite the eyes when you sleep.
Bees chase you and sting when you touch them.
Ugly politics sting wholesome lives,
even if you don't touch them,
even if you don't say a word against them.
Time knows man deceives man.
Ask Karl Marx for the reasons.

Rodin in the museum
sits thinking
hand under chin.

What's the relationship between thought and man?
Between thought and word?
Between pain and body?
How are water and land related?

9

Until now,
the language of all bedrooms at midnight
is the same.
The time when two bodies are united.
When the two hands of the clock
are eager to lie over each other.
The time when newer and newer dreams
breathe life in the skin.
The time when Spring comes down,
dances on bodies
singing like a bird
with the fresh fragrance of youth.
The time when plants grow

into trees, blossom
and bear fruit in a fraction of a second
and give an entirely new meaning
to time.
The time you pluck a flower from a tree
and wear it in your hair
and embrace the other,
press closer and closer.
The time when you shake the sky-tree
and fill your eyes with the sparkle of stars.
The time you burn incense
unseen and unheard by despair—
incense that silently burns
and sings songs of blue perfume.

This may be the story of a room,
a hut or a sidewalk.
Man hugs his woman to his heart.
A child grabs its mother's breast.
But no, this isn't true.

That moment,
agony is the only thing real.
The cry of distress is real.
The wooden horse knows but doesn't tell.
The ocean knows.
The blood you don't see on the waves knows.

The salty sea
forces into its embrace
all the sweet waters of rivers,
drinks to its full
and fattens itself
like a huge boa constrictor.
It twists and turns

and covers
time, the globe, and the faces of the poor,
the trees, the birds, and the entire world of animals
with a shroud of darkness and strangles them
with ropes of water,
stings them with its serpent waves
and laughs
ugly, hissing, dancing,
this ocean that can't quench the
thirst of people
when they are alive.

What you see now are not waves
but heaps of bodies
and threads of breath
cut off from bodies.

And silence.
Beyond the sun
crushed like a chicken egg
under the wild waves of the ocean
that rose—
beyond the moon
burnt black in the fire
of thunder and lightning—
beyond the stars left scattered
like rice on a leaf plate in the garbage dump
torn by fighting dogs, pigs, and hungry human skeletons—
beyond the sayings from texts
spread like a jungle all over the world—
beyond prayers,
beyond treachery,
beyond the wild laughter of the traitor,
beyond murder—
a silence larger than life,

larger than light,
larger than sound,
larger than speed.
A silence that pervades the universe
and settles in the eye of the corpse.

10

Ocean, do you remember,
when I was young,
you spread around my feet
with your white foam
like a little white furry dog?
When you licked my feet
with your wavy tongue,
I thought you were an innocent fellow.
I wanted to bring you home
and console you
in your agonizing roar,
make you my friend.

Yes, I wanted to console the ocean.
But I didn't know waves have fangs.
I didn't notice the wings of the wind are sharp like knives.
I didn't realize politics can flow into tears.

That minute,
the oceanic minute
when the sun and moon turned
into burnt coal,
everything ended.
All living beings
that trusted the earth and sky
turned into corpses.

Wooden Horse

It doesn't matter
whether the dead had an address.
It doesn't matter how many people
that moved from village to village,
belly in hand
for a morsel of food,
died.
That a banyan tree that gave shade
for a hundred years has been uprooted.
That birds dropped dead from the speed of the gale.
That electric poles were bent like plants.

The helpless scream of the world
shivered in the dark deadly embrace of water
and reached unknown islands of death.
Eyelids fluttered like the wings of helpless birds.
Arms struggled to protect throats from the watery sword
and were broken.
Man, bird, and beast stand alike,
heads bent
before death.
All the corpses
stand in silent testimony
to the neglect of those
who promised life
and rode their shoulders.

But never mind.
A skeleton doesn't demand
answers.

II

How can anyone kill anyone
a second time?

The minute God was born,
the minute they said your fate
is written on your forehead—
in that minute the human being died,
human action died.

How can anyone kill anyone now?
How can the ocean kill again?
Who can the wooden horse kill again?

Not to worry,
there are enough politicians
who compete among themselves
to serve the people.
There may not be enough crows,
vultures, hawks,
to clean up the corpses.
But there are contractors.
They'll serve the nation.

Don't worry a bit.
A homeless corpse
doesn't ask questions.

When the people who have wrapped themselves in power
all their life die,
the flag that flies over the country
bends its head low in sadness and respect.
The flag does not shed a tear
when people who lived with no cloth
to cover themselves,
who lived in dust,
return to dust.
It flies all the more proud

challenging the wind,
laughing at the sky.

No sad music is played.
Time's voice isn't choked.
No tears fill History's eyes.

Take comfort.
The living do not speak the truth.
Relax.
The corpse cannot talk.
When a person dies,
language dies
the world dies
God dies.

Sometime in the future
when these barren lands are plowed,
a skull appears
and laughs.

Don't be afraid.
A skeleton doesn't ask questions.

You're born in this world
only to be cheated.
You grow up only to be cheated.
You love only to be cheated.
You trust only to be cheated.

Death waits for you at every turn.
Not just at the end.
In ignorance,
in stupidity,

in the fear of life,
in living a double life,
in cunning politeness,
every minute
there's death.

But then there's science
to conquer death.
Let's plant plastic trees on the sidewalk,
plastic birds on plastic branches,
plastic ears of corn to show crops yield gold.
Let's make machine men and machine women,
then wind them up and leave them on beaches
so they can play and sing and live happily.
We will drink plastic milk from the plastic udders
of plastic cows.
We shall carry the wooden horse in rhythm
on our shoulders
all our life.

12

Jesus knows who betrays him
at the last supper.
I know who the murderers are.
I take the blame on myself.

No rockets for me.
No moon travel.
No airplanes.
I don't want politics that soil
life and time.
No trains, no buses,
I don't want the rush of this civilization.

Wooden Horse

I will take my tools from the paleolithic age
and go into the dark caves of History.
I will bury these corpses,
the carcasses of all the animals,
in myself.
I will invent a fuel
to burn the wooden horse.

I will weave a new cloth
with new dreams, new hope, new life
and come back
to clothe the human being,
naked, helpless,
alone
in the space between directions.

Generations

∾ SIVA REDDY

Next to the gate
stands a little boy
a three year old
a little afraid

His mother washes dishes
inside

His father
breaks stones
somewhere

He too
when he was a kid
stood at the gate

Another gate
if not this

Raped Poem

〜 BHAIRAVAYYA

I am a raped poem.
A ghost of a poem violated in the middle of the street.
I am a song of desire
crushed under the steel thighs of self-seekers.
My breasts were left
wounded to decay
from the cruel bites and scratches
of pretenders who are never satiated by their fucking fame.
I am a poem.

They laugh obscenely
and steal from other's work
to fulfill their cheap lust.
They killed me when I was still in my
mother's womb.
I am a putrified fetus.

Their ambition is to mask
their devilish faces
with delicate images
in print.
I am a body walked all over.

Drained of beauty
I reflect ugliness.

I am a poem.

Raped
crudely, obscenely
openly
shamelessly
in public view.
I've no skill, no refinement.

I am a raped poem
a painted ghost.

DEVIANT
SENTENCES

But even if I should want to be Sita,
I would never want to be Rama's wife.

Let's Go to Hell

∾ SRIRANGAM NARAYANA BABU

Come,
my love,
come with me to Hell.

The ritualists who worship
Indra,
and the romantics
who buzz like bees
about love, lost to life—

both misled you,

Woman, come
to Hell with me.

If there is a Heaven,
we will go there some other time.

Hell, they say,
doesn't last long.

Come with me
to Hell.

Come with me.
I'll have the river *Vaitarani*
cleaned up with phenol.

Let's Go to Hell

I'll have the roads in Hell
paved with DDT
and take you for a walk
in luxury.

I'll have eucalyptus trees planted
and wash your feet in
their oil.

Those cows
the dead hang on to by their tails
to cross the *Vaitarani*
and reach Heaven—
I'll cut their tails,
milk the cows
and make coffee for you.

I will give up games with meters
and have games of love played
in boiling oil.

I'll tear up the books
Chitragupta keeps
and give them to the grocer
to pack his snacks.

That buffalo the god of death
uses as a his vehicle,
I will put him to work on
farm land.

Heaven is selfish.
Heaven is evil.
Hell is real.
Hell helps us.

Sita

∾ PATHABHI

Sita was my classmate.
She and I pored over
that great new poem the *Ramayana*
of Satyanarayana.

When we were finished I asked her,
looking at her thoughtful eyes:

"You listened to the whole story.
We followed Rama
with the swiftness of poetry
into the wilderness of ancient time.
We met him, went to the forest with him; we saw him
kill Vali from behind the tree
and test his wife by fire.
Now tell me, do you really want to
live like Sita, the wife of the hero
Rama?"

When she heard me, she said:
"Hey, Pathabhi,
Sita is the very epitome of
Indian womanhood.
It's a dream, having
the good fortune
to live like her.

Sita

But even if I should want to be Sita,
I would never want to be Rama's wife.
Tell me, would you ever want to be Rama
yourself?"

"Why would I, when you don't want
to be Rama's wife?
My desire, rather,
is to become Ravana.

With all my ten mouths
I will kiss your lips, your face. I will bind you
with the gaze of my twenty eyes.
I will press you to my chest
with twenty strong arms
and make you one with me
in a tight embrace."

Now,
Sita is my wife.

Workers in Love

∾ KAVIKONDALA VENKATARAO

Sweat all over their faces,
heavy ropes on their shoulders,
they walk knee deep in dust.

Why do they sing of a necklace of beads,
and of coral on heavy breasts?

Crushed under the weight of iron,
all they think of is food.
They're out of breath as they go uphill.
Why do they sing of legs and anklets?
Of a heartthrob at the sound of feet?

They tighten their loincloths.
Tie up their hair.
Stop to catch their breath.

Why do they sing of love at first sight
and of waiting for the beloved by the bush?

No woman in sight.
No time to get excited.
Can't let go of the work at hand.

What fun do the workers have
in singing love
without love?

Sex Everywhere

∽ SRIRANGAM NARAYANA BABU

Stop your pretenses
you wise men.

Your noses
fuck your glasses
on the soft bed of your lashes.

The milk pot
and the churning rod
do it all the time
in the corner of your kitchen.

You forbid your widows
even to look at flowers.
But look into their bedrooms—
the sipping spoon and the water pot
are making love over there.

Your vegetables are rotting,
but the meat and tomato live in sin.

Stop your pretenses
you wise men.

Or
roll up the earth
and take it with you.

Throw the ocean out of the earth, or
drink it up, to the last drop.

The stars you see there,
squish them with your thumb.

Smash the moon,
so gods' women will not
use it as their mirror.

Let the king of gods be angry,
the god of gods be furious,
or, Shiva open his third eye.

You sure are capable of
doing this.

Donkeys in Anantapur

∽ ISMAIL

Two donkeys stand
meditating for hours.

They're always together
but never face each other.
One stands looking this way,
and the other looking that way.

"You look to the east
and I'll look west.
Who knows where wisdom dawns."

Suddenly, he brays,
runs in circles a couple of times
and returns to the same spot.

The other donkey doesn't move.
He doesn't even ask what happened.
He's sure that wisdom dawns
only in the east.

This World, Poor Thing

∾ REVATI DEVI

Left to myself,
I
would have been open
but if I were,
this barren virgin world,
they fear,
would get pregnant.

I
would have been holy
but if I were,
this useless virgin world,
they fear,
would turn around and get laid.

I
would have been pure
but if I were,
this old-maid world,
they fear,
would go and get married.

That's why
I am
untruthful
unclean
unholy.

Moon in China Bazaar

∽ PATHABHI

The moon is put up
on the sky in China Bazaar, up on the top,
unnecessarily, unatrociously.

Look down here, an endless flow of life,
a crazy crowd. People, cars,
man, machine,
rubbing shoulders, running mad.
No one looks at you, moon, even by mistake.
People have no taste for the white sweet creamy drink
you give for free.
The music that sounds in our ears—and hearts as well—
is the ringing of the silver rupee.

Sorry, moon. What can I say?
No one even mistakes you for a lost rupee coin.
Really, you are not wanted here.

Our eyes are dazzled by the glitter of
electric lights,
the mad dance of neon
advertisements.
We like those electric bulbs that change shape
every minute.
But you, unlucky moon,
you take fifteen days to change your shape.
Too long, too slow.

You'll lose to your competition in
attracting people's attention.
You'll go broke.
We have no use for you here.

We just don't like your dull round face
the poets made such a big deal of.
We salivate at those painted faces of fashionable women.
We want to grab them with our greedy eyes and eat them up.

You can't get along with the sky in China Bazaar.
You look like a village oaf
who lost his way and entered Spencer's.

Moon, you are not wanted here.

Me?

∽ NIRASANA KAVULU

When I was young
I was my father's daughter.
I was my younger brother's elder sister.

When I grew up, when I matured,
I was my father-in-law's daughter-in-law;
his respected son's wife.
I was my sons' mother.

When I grew old, no longer menstruating,
I was his daughter's grandma,

a female thing.

Once every five years,
in the election manifestoes,
I am a slogan,
quite fashionable.

Police Report

∾ DEVARAKONDA BALAGANGADHARA TILAK

The report is in.
A. K. Rao's death
is untimely. He died
a natural death.
No plot, no poisoning.

But then it is bad manners to die
in an expensive hotel, in room number thirteen
on the third floor, in the middle of a meeting.

If he was there on office work,
dying before finishing his job
may be a dereliction
of duty.

Since he walked up three flights of stairs
(he feared moving up, never asked for a lift)
the faithful heart of this faithful man
probably rebelled and stopped.

In any case, his death is a fact.
He did not stand up to salute when his boss came,
which is a more definite proof of death
than the doctor's report.

Nothing about his life is suspicious.
He was a clerk, his father was a clerk and his grandfather was a clerk.

Police Report

His family was traditionally obedient and respectfully poor.
He had six children, an old mother, an ill-fed cat
and one wife weak and pale.

He rented a portion of a house
with one and a half rooms, a bath—
it had holes in the walls—and an attic.

He wore red shirts, but was not a communist.
He walked in alleys, but was no surrealist.
He laughed and talked to himself, but he was not a philosopher.
He looked at the sky as if he was lost in dreams, but he was no poet,
     no way.

He paid the milkman and the grocer on time every month
and at the month's end he and his wife starved because they had
no money left to eat.
Occasionally, he went to watch a free street play.
He did not know why people get VD's, he didn't even smoke *bidis*.

Once a year he went to a movie and stood at the end of the line.
He was not a member of any group, political, social, not one.
He voted for whomever his boss told him and every week he prayed.
He never accepted a bribe, never abused any one,
he was always gentle and good.
He was absolutely moral, totally truthful, and patriotic to the core.

But the day before his death he met a friend named Kanakayya and
     asked:
"What's happiness, how does it feel, and how do you find it?"

This is a blemish on his life, which was otherwise totally clean.
The country is safe, he's dead before he asked,
"What does all this mean?"

Forces of Production

∾ NIRASANA KAVULU

Darling,
we are Forces of Production.
We must produce.
The Red Book exhorts us
to nationalize our resources.

Don't ever doubt
that the fruit of your womb is
Surplus Value.
Surrender it at the feet of the Party.
You're the true goddess of courage.

Those who joined us in matrimony,
know them as the Capitalists.
They robbed us of our hopes with stolen gifts.
Get rid of them.
Our true love has only one aim:
The welfare of the People.

Don't ask me to talk
of love sweet as honey,
to denounce empty polemics.
The southern breeze and love
are bourgeois terms.
They catch you unawares,
like the net catches fish.

Forces of Production

The sun rises in the east
like a red flag with a thousand rays.
Let's go on our pilgrimage
to Moscow and Beijing
to see our leaders,
the gods of our hearts.

WOMEN TAKE THE WORLD

I will close this dark chapter
and come out:
Rainbow on a blue sky.

A Birth

REVATI DEVI

with the fragrance of twenty-five bodies burning with desire
with the beauty of five snow-clad mountain ranges
with the moving music of infinite pairs of stellar bodies
with the love of a thousand brilliant dark eyes
with the cool rays of a billion moons
with two valleys red with passion
with a hundred joys of the soft, green grass
with a trillion stars of sparkling looks
with the thirst of forty youthful suns
with a single heart, for a single heart

now I'm born.

Qaus-e Qazah*

∾ SHAJAHANA

You fear

I will run away with someone
and ruin your religion.

So you put me in this prison, this veil.

Wherever life flows,
you build walls across it
with broken glass on top.

You can say *talak*, thirty times if you so desire,
and marry
again and again and again.
Open adultery pure and perfect.
Allah the merciful will not punish you.

But I
should live like a rat in a hole,
a lone ghost in your dark hallway
and remain,
the fifth leg on your bed of pleasures.

* Rainbow

Even the night shrouded by darkness
looks out for morning.

I am transferring my silence to you.

Here is my veil, my upper cloth
which I tore into pieces.
Make a quilt and roll on it.

I will close this dark chapter
and come out:
Rainbow on a blue sky.

Birds Love the Net

∾ KONDEPUDI NIRMALA

Your first question
as you come through the doorway:
Where's my son-in-law?

Second question:
Aren't the kids home yet?

Third question:
The house is all messy, why don't you
keep it clean?

I try hard to place my face
in every corner your eyes fall on.

Doesn't help.
You too care more for the housewife
than for me.

Suppressing the sighs
of the river renamed at every shore,
this hen, your mother of chicks,
scratches words in front of you.

Mom, I am your daughter.
Won't you ask
why your child is so old already?
Why did she run away from your lap so soon?

No, it is not the hair graying behind the ears,
the hollowing eyes,
the rules of society,
not even the restless fury
whirling round and round,
trying to bite off the tether.

Whenever we see each other,
the gate is closed at the crossing.

The train cuts across our painful smiles
clanking, fuming.
We let the thousand and one heads and hands pass.
We stop helpless.

We forget in the noise
the rush of our blood in the veins.
I take care not to let
my thoughts blot the letters I write.
You take the answers
to the three questions you have.

My words melt in my mouth.
My childhood dies in me.
My ocean becomes
a center for smugglers.

Once again my name is entered
among the birds that love their net.

Physical Geography

∾ MAHE JABEEN

The moment I am told
it will burn me,
I want to embrace the sun.
Just once.

That's how I am.
I always want to do
what's prohibited.

I erase boundaries.
The sky is my limit.

I lifted the veils of waves
of blue seas
and studied the freedom of water.

I swam against the current
and joined the battle
of the waves against the ocean.

Now I have to go get the essence
of the thundering clouds
and rub it into the vocal chords
of my people.

Sometime soon
I will occupy the ocean
and sow my dreams in it.

Ideal Wife

∾ MAHE JABEEN

I am Masjid
He is Mandir

We named our son Jesus

Ayodhya was never a problem for us

That it was not a problem for us
was a problem for them

They talked
my heart was wounded
They looked
my body was wounded

I learned to protect myself from the wounds

I left my caste
forgot my religion
walked into the open
dreamed of a new life

But I didn't know
that religion follows you like a shadow
Tradition hounds you like a dog

Ideal Wife

I didn't wear my *tali* on my neck
I didn't wear a *bottu* on my forehead
They decided these were terrible crimes

I did not count my husband as one of my gods
but treated him as my friend
That was included among the strange events of the world

We avoid the life they wish for us
a quarreling, arguing, sleeping routine
They don't understand our life
of meeting occasionally
living separately

I do not want a Nobel prize
for being an ideal wife

Fall

∼ MAHE JABEEN

He always did that.

I asked him to come alone
and he brought an entire spring with him.

Trees were parading outside
in the silence of the leaves.
The sky froze in the stream.
I remember vaguely
stars melting as they fell down.

No.
Take the moonlight
and the full moon.
Just give my Sun back to me.

Let this dark night pass in waiting for him.

He always did that.
He brought the songs of birds with him.

In his presence
I regained my lost childhood.
My body turned into a school of senses.
I slept hiding myself in his heart.

Fall

He woke me
mercilessly in the middle of the night
and told me how guns chased the sounds of the river.
I hid him in my heart
out of fear.

He is no more.

He fell somewhere
in the recent fall
that came out of season.

FROM THE MARGINS TO
THE MAIN STAGE

*I was counted out,
but to tell the truth
we were all sons
of the same mother.*

I Was One of Them

∽ JASHUVA

A man from my country spoke to the world
assembly of religions and they approved.
A merchant from my land defied the powers
of five continents with a spindle.
A scholar from my home sat on the highest
teacher's chair in the land of the whites.
A poet of my people won the honor
of all the world, the Nobel prize.
It was our man who told you trees have feelings
and proved it all with scientific evidence.

I was counted out,
but to tell the truth
we were all sons
of the same mother.

The Bat Messenger

∽ JASHUVA

He is innocent, so he is happy
with what little he earns.
He is hungry, so he forgets his cares
if he has a meal.
He lives in a space with only
the four directions to protect him.
He is an untouchable,
the last-born son
of India that is Bharat.

He lives south of Thanjavur
the city once famous
for the great king who supported
Telugu poets.

He makes shoes
to protect the feet of his masters
who keep him poor
and keep him low.

If he doesn't work the land
it will yield no crop.
He sweats all day to feed the world
but doesn't have food to eat.

In a country where people feed
snakes milk

and ants sugar,
even the goddess of justice stays away
from where this poor man lives.

God shows no compassion,
not to mention men.
No one has ever told him what
he did to deserve his fate.

The anti-goddess Poverty
sucks his blood for pleasure.
The four-hooded snake of Hindu castes
hisses at him if he comes close.

All day he works hard
and returns home in the evening.
He has his gruel and rests
when a bat enters his house.

It moves like a piece of darkness
that has a nose and a face of its own.
Its flapping wings blow out
the blinking lamp in the corner.

He begins to speak to the bat
of his life and all his troubles.
Who else will listen to him
if not birds, beasts, and insects?

"You live in temples—
an honor
denied to people like us.
Welcome to you, sacred bat.
I hope you're well
in your penance of hanging

The Bat Messenger

upside down
with your family and friends.

This is the house of an untouchable.
What have you come here for?
You dine in the company of gods
but you come where there's no food.

You come from a line of sages
who gave their lives for the world.
Bird, I bow to you.
Would you do me a favor?

The world sleeps this night in peace.
I'm here abandoned
as if I have
an incurable
contagious disease.

You're a bird and also a beast.
The world is confused about you.
You're a bad omen to them.
For me you are a friend.
Would you take my message
to that god
in Banaras?

They shut my mouth
with their karma theory
and steal my food from me.
Could you ask god to show me
what my karma was?

When you hang from the ceiling in the temple
you are close to god's ears.

Gentle bat, tell my woes to god
when the priest is not around.

Come back and tell me please
what the god of gods has said.
I have no one else to turn to
for help
or support.

My home has no doors to close.
It's always open to you.
You don't have to knock
day or night.
You're always welcome here."

The Wall

~ ISMAIL

I know what should be out
and what should be in.
But then
what's this window doing here?

A Child Is Born

∾ SATISH CHANDAR

Why only boulders across the graves?
Let them line up whole mountains.
Surely, a Jesus will rise
in an explosion of light
like the morning sun.

A cemetery in the middle of the village
casts out the whole population!

Four sides to the village.
Four legs to an animal.
Four rows for crossing.
Caste walks on four feet.

Somewhere, far on the fifth side
a two-legged child is born in a manger.
I don't know whether a comet appeared,
but a tail broke off.

Cattle get angry that they are polluted
by the touch of the child's feet.
They cry, bray, bark, and howl.

This child is the hope of the slave.
The dream of a century.
The first word of the song of freedom.

A Child Is Born

But according to the law of the cattle
the birth of this child is bad.

It's against the law to have two feet.
They drive nails so he shall not walk.
It's against the law to have two hands.
They drive holes so he shall not ask for work.

It's against the law to have a brain.
They stick a crown of thorns on his head
so he shall not write a constitution again.

It's against the law to have a lovely face.
They spit on him so no mother can kiss him.

More particularly,
it is against the law to have a heart.
They drive spears in his chest.
A son of a slave shall not love.

The child is killed on the cross
in the open rice fields.
The sun sets at high noon.
The sky splits into five pieces.
The sun covers his face with four of the pieces
stitched together.

The last words of the child on the cross:
"Father they *know* what they are doing,
keep them alive until I come back."

The cattle run away from the village.
Mother Earth is pregnant
right where the four streets meet.
All the heroes' graves are pregnant.

Timid people.
They ban animal killing
even before the child rises.
"The child shall come to this world
to search for and kill the animals."

Mothers, heavy with grief for the loss of your children,
welcome him in white clothes.

A child is born.
Hallelujah.

A Birth Postponed

∾ SATISH CHANDAR

My son always asks this question:
"Father, when should I be born?"

As I stand before the mirror
I don't see the shape of my limbs,
but a series of abuses.

I see my thick curly hair
and recall my great-grandfather's long
hair tied up, rejected by razors,
scissors.

I fiercely press my hair down with a tough comb.

My ears hide their fiery music
like two earthen lamps.

I fear that I have done something wrong
and pull my hair and cover my ears
to protect them from molten lead.

As my closed lips
gently begin to smile
I remember the cups of poison
given to my ancestors

by upper caste women
as gifts of broken love.

I throw up—kisses—on my image in the mirror.

When I button my long-sleeve shirt
I remember the wind
that clothed my mother's bosom
from all the way to the end of the village.

I feel my shoulders one after the other
again and again.

As I put my nice-looking belt around my waist,
I feel that someone is trying to tie a broom behind me
to get me to sweep away my own history.

I search to make sure there are no loops on the belt.

When I tie the laces on my shining shoes,
I hear my father's feet,
kissed only by Mother Earth.
I hear him moan with the pain from his corns.

I bow to my own feet and stand up.

When I finally want to lift my head and stroke my mustache,
I hear my boss mutter with his merit and talent,
"Low-caste recruits, what are you proud of?"

I try hard to swallow the future of the past.

My son has only one question.
"Father, when should I be born?"

A Birth Postponed

I move away from the mirror,
pick up my grandfather's drum hanging from the wall,
and beat it like mad.

An acoustic abortion occurs
and a birth gets postponed.

Birthmark

༄ KHADAR MOHIUDDIN

A certain fiction bit me
  a distortion
    a slander

August 10, 1955
that's the day I was born

  in a small village
  in a remote corner in Krishna District

Long before I was born
  my name was listed among traitors

History depicted
  son as stepson,
    divided brother from brother
and left me alone

Textbooks laughed at me
  in my childhood

I was just becoming a person
when this history drove strange fears
  deep into me
    tortured me, threw me
      to the howling winds

Birthmark

The present makes me responsible
   for things I've nothing to do with

The present casts around me
   shadows of suspicion

Shadows watching me
     over my head
       always, all ways

They squeeze my existence into numbers

They see 1947
   in the umbilical cord, freshly cut
     its end still wet with the blood
       of the baby born in my house

   Hindi—Hindu—Hindustan
   Muslim go to Pakistan

   Another place to go as well
   You will know its name as hell

Helpless in the theater of slogans
   I'm imprisoned in the present

No constitution pats my back
The throne of three lions
     smiling behind their whiskers
      takes no notice of me

I have no human form
   except as an alien
     as some kind of memorial to 1947

in the mind
of the first class citizen

Yes, I'm a conspirator
aren't I?

It's no conspiracy to identify
Islam with Islamabad
It's no conspiracy to dig up
the earth under my feet
It's no conspiracy
to make me a refugee
in the very country of my birth
It's no conspiracy
to poison the air I breath
and the space I live in
It's certainly no conspiracy
to cut me to pieces
and then imagine an uncut Bharat

My religion is a conspiracy
my prayer-meetings are a conspiracy
my lying quiet is a conspiracy
my attempt to wake up is a conspiracy
my desire to have friends is a conspiracy
my desire to live is a conspiracy
my ignorance, my backwardness, a conspiracy

If I marry, it is a conspiracy
If I have kids, it is a conspiracy

I sell flowers on the sidewalk
for a morsel of rice
I sell fruits, peanuts
Fix broken umbrellas, watches

Birthmark

Sew clothes on porches
Card cotton
   to live in peace
       in quiet

But suddenly
my blood flows in the streets
   like a river that purifies them

Before an election,
   before all sorts of events,
      my blood directs the future of this country

My blood
provides the magic touch
   that flies the candidates
      right into the Parliament hall

It paves the way
   for real estate

It's the armor
   of political power

It's the assuring hand
   that raises them to positions

My blood becomes the auspicious dot
   on Mother India's forehead
      the red lotus to be worshipped

Every step I put forward
   turns into a pool of blood

My house fuels their fireworks
My house burns for their festivals
My house turns into the ashes of their demon
on every Divali

The dove's eggs
    the ancient man preserved for future generations
        in history's nest
            are crushed

I hear the echo
  of Mother Earth's breaking ribs
      for the last time

I dream no more in my mother tongue
My thoughts take form in the language of the masters
Cricket matches weigh and measure my patriotism

Never mind my love for my motherland
What's important
  is how much
      I hate the other land

My role as an evil-clown-antagonist
entertains the audience
    on the silver screen
        on the theater stage
It leaves me handicapped

Forgive me, friends
I can't revere your great poet
    when he makes up new words
        to disfigure me

Birthmark

I am not moved by the
passion of the people's singer
   He sees no difference between
      the Muslim tyrant
        and the Muslim poor

When they talk of me
   as a synonym for violence
      and a symbol of intolerance
        I laugh it off

When they tell you
   cycles of demon stories
      to warn you of your future with me
        I laugh it off

When the rulers' watchdogs
   bark history into religion,
   turn religion into history
      I laugh it off

But what I hear in response is slander

No, mine is not really a laugh
   It's a cry of pain
      that I swallow day after day
Article 370
   and the barbed wire of personal law:
      They strangle me
I am the victim

Secularism in words
   unconcerned with action
      kills me
Again, I am the victim

I know you've said my birth was blemished
That's my birthmark

What's this affinity between the rulers' strategies
    and the rope that tightens around my neck?

Why does the stream of my blood flow
    between the two pieces of land
        they secretly divided among themselves
    like a boundary agreed upon?

I shouldn't ask

On the tips of the tridents
    on the bayonets of the police
        on the ballot boxes
my birthmark sheds blood

I can't question why

Yes, my birthmark is me
    my existence, my citizenship

It's my ancestral property
        inherited from the earth
            the sky, the air
                the surroundings I live in

It's a wound that never heals

Prayer

∾ AFSAR

1–3

We praise only you. We cringe with shame like crumbs
of food thrown into empty hands.
Lord, we lost our world.

We fall through the leftover soup dripping from the beggar's arms.
Our fruit has gone bad.

4–7

We adore only you. We pierce our eyes looking toward your face we
can not see.
We have no other way.

No favors are shown to us, only fury.

We lose our way on paths untrodden,
over and over.

1–5

No, we have no doubts in our mind.
We save our fears.

We know everything we see is a lie; so we believe in what we don't
  see.
Every day we unite, because we have to.

Now that we know no one gives us anything,
we don't draw a big distinction between the truth and a lie.

We behave as if we believe.

But we know for sure
nothing is certain except this world.

Talk of fulfillment?
People die. Power changes hands.

6–7

We are sealed. They sealed our hearts, shut our ears with promises.
Mosques fall right in front of our eyes. Yet, we sleep in peace.

Those who force us back to sleep if we are up before sunrise,
who wake up startled from sleep at the midday call for prayer,
who sleep, as if nothing ever bothered them, evening, night or day—

they should be punished.

Don't you think so,
God?

What Do I Want?

MADDURI NAGESHBABU

I want a little breeze
a glass of water
some warmth
a little sky in this dungeon
a little land for me in this country of mine

Will you give it?

I want a life where I don't have to move away
where I can walk without having to cringe
I want the food that Manu has stolen from my plate
I want those curtains of separation to go
More particularly
I want my throne back

Will you give it?

I want these clouds lifted
I wants these walls shattered
I want this silence to break
I want this stickiness to be washed away

Man
I want real citizenship
Will you give it?

I want a touch
I want you to shake my hand with your heart
I want a bond of blood between my colony and your village
I want this empty space that divides us filled

More particularly
I want the dead bodies of your gods
Will you give them to me?

I want a human being out of
you, who are caught in the cactus of texts
I want valleys of love along the flow of your life
I want your kiss free from your levels of high and low
an embrace free from aggression
I want union with you
Will you give it?

What do I want?
I want you
I want room in your heart
I want to eat in your house
I want you to come to my hut and talk marriage
with my daughter for your son
I want us to be family

Friend, I want this country to be ours
This land should be leveled for us to walk
without ups and downs

Do you want to come?

Black and White

〜 MACHIRAJU SAVITHRI

We worshipped dark
Krishna. He was our deity, our
supreme god.
We worshipped the dark woman
Parvati, Draupadi,
mother of the Universe,
the temptress of the world,
our ultimate beauty.

We fought against
the white government
and their racist rule.
We called the leader of the struggle
Mahatma,
great soul.

We honored King, the leader
who led his black people to fight
peacefully. We called him
another Gandhi.

Today our gods are not black.
We paint them in shades of blue
or make them white.
We come to King's country
and look down on blacks.

Are we still slaves at heart
craving for whiteness
even after the white rule ended?

Or are we colorblind
thinking we are white so we can
join the whites
to get rich
in their country?

NOTES

A HISTORICAL
AFTER-ESSAY

INDEX

NOTES

Names of poets are listed in alphabetical order with a brief biographical note. Following the biographical information are the titles of the poet's poems included in this anthology in alphabetical order with the page numbers where they appear. The title of each poem is followed by its source information, which includes 1) its original title, or the first line of the original in case there is no title, 2) the year of composition, if known, in parentheses, and 3) the publication from which the poem is taken.

∽ ABBURI RAMAKRISHNA RAO (1896–1979)

Rāmakrishna Rao studied at Sanskrit College in Mysore and the University of Calcutta. He went to Santiniketan, the famous school of Rabindranath Tagore, but did not feel comfortable with the Tagore worship prevailing there. He returned to Andhra and worked as a librarian at Andhra University in Waltair. Ramakrishna Rao was an engaging conversationalist and made many friends among younger poets. He was active in many fields and creatively influenced every field he entered. For some time he worked with M. N. Roy organizing the Radical Humanist movement in Andhra. Later, he organized a theater group and traveled all over Andhra producing plays. He was one of the architects of the Andhra Pradesh Sāhitya Akaḍĕmi, a literary academy sponsored by the state government. Many poets, among whom Sri Sri was the most prominent, considered Ramakrishna Rao as their mentor. Ramakrishna Rao wrote little, and many of his poems were lost because he did not pay attention to saving his work.

The Farmer's Song (42)

"Kāpu pāṭa," (1918) *Ūhāgānamu, Itarakṛtulu* (New Delhi: Kavita, 1973; second printing, Hyderabad: Abburi Trust, 1994)

This poem is known for its craftsmanship and lyricism, hallmarks of the Bhāvakavitvam poets who romanticize village life.

A Longing (76)

"Nene kādu ...," ibid.

Selected from a longer poem of several verses, this single verse has received attention for its deeply religious tone.

◌ ADIVI BAPIRAJU (1895–1952)

Poet, painter, dancer, and novelist, Bapiraju represents an unusual combination of skills. His poems are artless, effortless expressions of a movement or a feeling. He sang them as songs, often unmindful of time or melody. His poems are few, but they are all energetic in their use of words and tone. Bapiraju is remembered as a passionate advocate for the revival of the past glory of Telugu art. He taught painting at Āndhra Jātiya Kaḷāśāla (Andhra National College), Machilipatnam, Krishna district. Oswald Couldrey, who worked as principal of the Arts College at Rajahmundry, was his mentor and compared him to Endymion of Greek mythology. Apparently Bapiraju loved that comparison and wrote a song about it. Bapiraju was affectionately called *Bāpi-bāva*, Brother-in-law Bapi, by the poets of the period.

Steps (77)

"Mĕṭlu," *Vaitāḷikulu* (1935; sixth printing, Vijayawada: Adarsa Grantha Mandali, 1966)

It's characteristic of Bapiraju that he allows his subject to chose its meter. The meter of this poem concretely presents the long flight of ascending steps to many a Hindu temple in India.

◌ AFSAR (b. 1964)

Careful in his use of words, in poetry as well as in prose, Afsar received his Ph.D. in Telugu literature and worked for a number of years for *Āndhra Bhūmi*, a Telugu newspaper. Currently, he teaches Telugu at the

University of Wisconsin–Madison while pursuing graduate studies. The poem included in this anthology is best appreciated when read with the suras of the Koran, corresponding to the numbers given with each of the stanzas.

Prayer (232)
   "Ajā" (1997), *Jaljalā* (Nallagonda: 1998)

~ AJANTA (1929–1998)
Perhaps the only poet in Telugu who was recognized as a major poet as soon as he published his first poem. His "Cĕṭlu Kūlutunna Dr̥śyam" (A Scene of Falling Trees) made a powerful impression on contemporary literary taste for its perfect control of the free verse form, for its evocative diction and imagery. Critics still consider it the best poem in free verse. Ajanta wrote very infrequently but nearly everything he wrote was read and reread by his readers.

Ajanta, whose birth name is Penumarti Viswanatha Sastri, worked most of his active life as the editor of *Āndhra Prabha*, a Telugu daily. In 1993, his friends published a volume of his poems, *Svapna-lipi*, for which he rewrote, from his memory, all the poems he had published earlier in various journals. In the preface to that book Ajanta writes, "I don't keep copies of any of my published poems. I destroy them. There are no dates; every poem is now. Poetry doesn't need a calendar." Ajanta remained untouched by the massive literary movements of his time, and refused to be drawn into politics. In 1971, at the height of the popularity of Virasam (Revolutionary Writers Association), he declared that Telugu poetry was going through a dark age.

Dateline Hyderabad: 1990 December 8 (117)
   "Deṭlain Haidarabād, 1990 disembar 8," *Svapna-lipi* (Vijayawada: Kavitvam Pracuranalu, 1993)

Me on the Wall (122)
   "Māntrikuḍu," ibid.

Sleep (119)
   "Suśupti," ibid.

∾ ARUDRA (1925–1998)

Well-known by his pen name Arudra, Bhagavatula Sankara Sastri made an impressive contribution to Telugu poetry, literary history, criticism, journalism, and music. Scholars respect him for his thirteen-volume *Samagra Āndhra Sāhityam*, a comprehensive history of Telugu literature. The selection included here is from his *Tvamevā'ham,* a long poem in free verse, which made an impression on the literary community when his famous uncle, Sri Sri, introduced it with his approval. Arudra was active in the Marxist literary movement of Abhyudaya Racayitala Saṅgham, and continued to espouse a liberal ideology in all his writings.

Arudra is at his best in writing fun poems with end-rhymes and is compared to the American poet Ogden Nash. His *Iṇṭiṇṭi pajyālu* belongs to this vein.

Death of Man (106)

"Chirajīvi mānavunaku mṛtyuvu," (1948) *Tvamevā'ham* (1949; fourth edition, Vijayawada: Visalaandhra Publishing House, 1999)

∾ BAIRAGI (1925–1978)

Popularly known as Bairagi, Aluri Bairagi Chaudari is a lone writer who did not belong to any literary movement or group. He wrote in an intensely personal and tragic voice. His poems read like silent voices of lost travelers in a distant desert. Bairagi, who was also a good scholar of Hindi literature, never married, lived by himself, did odd jobs, and possessed no property. He ate very little, drank lots of tea, and smoked nonstop. He died a slow death from malnutrition.

Give Me Confidence (123)

"Nak'koncěm Nammakm'ivvu," *Āgama-gīti* (Madras: 1981)

The Telugu word for confidence is *nammakam*, which could also mean faith, belief, trust.

Who Is Awake in the Dead of Night? (110)

"Melukonnāvaḍu," ibid.

When it is night for everyone . . . : lines from the *Bhagavadgīta* 2–69

∾ BHAIRAVAYYA (b. 1942)

Bhairavayya, whose birth name is Mulukutla Manmohan Sahay, was a member of a group of rebel poets who called themselves Digambara Kavulu (Naked Poets). Later, he joined Nirasana Kavulu (see page 260).

Raped Poem (178)

"Cĕracabaḍḍa Gītānni," (1965): Rā (Hyderabad: 1970)

∾ CHAVALI BANGARAMMA (1897–1978)

One of the finest poets of the Bhāvakavitvam period, Bangaramma wrote very few poems, each of which haunts us with a sense of tragedy. Her images bring to mind the scenes of a vaguely remembered village. Her diction comes from the ordinary words women use in daily life. Her poems look gentle and innocent on the surface but take you to a deeply disturbing world. The first poem included here talks of a village pond, serene and placid, but intensely disquieting all the same. The hibiscus, a bush with bright red flowers, is evocative of femininity and brings to mind an image of a woman bending on the lake when she draws water from it. Further on the poem turns silently agitating, with images of trees running like snakes all over the lake, a shattered sky and a frightened sun. Very little is known about this remarkable poet. Histories of the literature of the period are silent about her.

Hibiscus on the Lake (52)

"Nīḍa," *Vaitālikulu*

bŏṭṭu: a mark on the forehead worn by a woman indicating that she is not a widow

My Brother (56)

"Anna," *Mahodayamu: Ādhunika Khaṇḍikā Samuccayamu,* ed. Sivasankara Sastri (Kakinada: Andhra Pracarini Ltd.,1949)

∾ CHELLAPILLA VENKATA SASTRI (1870–1950)

Chellapilla Venkata Sastri was a power to be reckoned with in the field of Telugu poetry during the first half of the twentieth century. He and his collaborator Divakarla Tirupati Sastri (1872–1920) toured all over the Telugu area speaking verses to their audiences. Together the twin poets were known as Tirupati-Venkata-kavulu. Their performances of oral versification were popularly known as *śatāvadhānas*, where the poets took questions and literary riddles from one hundred members of their audiences and extemporaneously responded to them in verse. The poets made Telugu poetry a household practice in Andhra during the early decades of the century. Venkata Sastri influenced a whole generation of modern poets, many of whom were his direct students. Most of his poems became part of the oral tradition and are quoted by educated people in conversations.

He was the only major poet in the century who did not know English, refused to be influenced by its power, and inaugurated a style of modernity distinct from the colonial modernity that followed him.

Venkata Sastri was known for his ability to stand up to anyone who found fault with his literary work. His fighting spirit became a part of literary culture in Telugu. The poem included here is what the poet said when his teacher, Sripada Krishnamurti Sastri, found errors of grammar in Venkata Sastri's poetry.

Born for Poetry (3)
    "kavanārthamb'udayiñcitin . . . ," from oral circulation

∾ DASU SRIRAMULU (1846–1908)
Dasu Sriramulu was a prolific writer whose satire about the subcastes of Brahmins of his time made him very popular. His descriptions of women from different castes in his *Tĕlugu Nāḍu,* with their accurate ethnographic detail, show his skill in bringing contemporary themes into poetry. His literary style was traditional, and he was critical of changes coming into society from the introduction of English education. A good musician himself, he wrote a number of erotic-devotional songs addressed to the deity Veṇugopālasvāmi of Eluru. Courtesans in the town used to learn from him and perform the songs during the Temple festivals. He knew several languages including English, Persian, and Sanskrit. He began as a teacher and then took a law degree and worked as an advocate.

The Other Tongue (4)
"mudi karaṇālu …," from oral circulation

∾ DEVARAKONDA BALAGANGADHARA TILAK (1922–1966)
Affectionately remembered as a master of lyricism and a poet who has
a concern for social justice and cultural progress, Tilak combines the
values of two ideologically opposed literary movements: Bhāvakavit-
vam and Abhyudayakavitvam, the former stood for aesthetic values
and the latter for political commitment. His mastery of free verse and
his ability to blend classical Sanskrit compounds into modern spoken
Telugu earned him a distinct place in the development of modern
poetry. A craftsman of refreshing imagery and a poet who refused to
remain tied to political ideologies, Tilak (who is not related to the
famous Maharashtra national leader of the same name) died young, at
the height of his literary productivity. His volume of poetry, *Amṛtam
Kurisina Rātri*, is a posthumous publication. Other publications of Tilak
include short stories and some well-crafted metrical verses.

The Night It Rained Life (147)
"Amṛtam Kurisina Rātri," (1962) *Amṛtam Kurisina Rātri* (Vijayawada:
Visalaandhra Publishing House, 1968)

Police Report (195)
"Si.ai.ḍi. Riporṭ," (1965) ibid.
A. K. Rao: The original has the complete name, Ayanapurapu
Subbaravu, ostensibly for its legalistic tone. The tone of the name also
suggests a faceless person, a nobody.

A Prayer (153)
"Prārthana," (1963) ibid.

∾ DEVULAPALLI KRISHNA SASTRI (1897–1980)
Revered as the greatest poet of the Bhāvakavitvam period, Krishna
Sastri had enormous influence on three decades of Telugu poets. His
charismatic personality and carefree lifestyle attracted a number of fol-
lowers who gathered around him wherever he went. Young poets of

his period adored him to the extent of imitating his dress and hair style. His first book of poems, *Krishna-pakṣamu*, generated a tempest of opposition from classicists. He toured all over Andhra and gave readings and talks on modern poetry. His talks paved the way for a whole new mode of modern literary appreciation.

Krishna Sastri's lyrical style defies translation. His romantic appeal, too, does not last beyond its Telugu context. Limitations such as these severely constrained the choice of poems from this very influential poet.

Her Eyes (34)

"Āmě Kannulu," *Vaitāḷikulu*

The poem is written in a meter called *āṭavěladi*, but reads like prose so the meter appears to work accidentally. A parody of the last line of the poem gained circulation as a joke about Krishna Sastri's poems. The last line in the original reads: *ědiyo apūrva raktima sphuriyiñcu kāni / arthammu kāni bhāva-gītammul'avi*. The parody reads *leni* instead of the second *kāni* and the line now means: "They are poems / that look as if they have a beauty you've never known before / but really they have no meaning."

The Palanquin (32)

"Pallaki," ibid.

O oho: Palanquin bearers chant "*O oho*" as they go to give them a rhythm in bearing the burden.

In Search of Krishna (35)

"Anveṣanamu," (1925) ibid.

With its glorification of love, Bhāvakavitvam found a rich theme in the Krishna legends from Hindu mythology. A number of poets of this period wrote on the Krishna theme. However, here Krishna is more a human lover than the dark lord of the mythology. Krishna Sastri writes this poem as a conversation between two *gopis*—cowherd girls—who find each other in the woods in the middle of the night, both of them looking for Krishna. The musical texture of the poem is so rich that words flow into one another, submerging their lexical identity and the metrical features as well. Published in *Vaitāḷikulu*, the anthology of Bhāvakavitvam poets, this poem is considered one of the best of Krishna Sastri's writings.

∾ DUVVURI RAMIREDDY (1895–1947)

A poet and scholar who mastered French, German, English, Tamil, Bengali, Urdu, Persian, and Sanskrit in addition to his native Telugu, Ramireddy was a quiet participant in the Bhāvakavitvam movement. He published a number of volumes of poetry and contributed to contemporary literary criticism, but avoided the limelight and stayed in his native village in southern Andhra. His *Pāna'sāla*, a translation of the Rubayyat of Omar Khayyam, from Persian is considered a good poem in its own right in modern Telugu literature. He is known for his imaginative depiction of village life in poetic works such as *Kṛṣīvaluḍu* (The Farmer). He wrote mostly in conventional meter, but the poem included in this anthology is atypical of his general style.

Tryst (46)

"Abhisārika," *Vaitāḷikulu*

A woman who goes out in disguise to meet her lover at a tryst is called *abhisārika* and is a frequent theme in Sanskrit love poetry.

∾ GURAJADA APPARAO (1862–1915)

The appearance of Halley's comet in 1910 had an important effect on the beginnings of modern poetry in Telugu. Conventional beliefs about the comet were negative, leading to fears of impending calamities such as the death of a king, drought, or famine. But Apparao saw the comet differently. Apparao's poem on the comet came to represent the beginnings of modernity in Telugu. He created a symbol of progress and change rather than calamity and doom from the comet's appearance. He rejected conventional Telugu meters, with fixed syllables and rules of caesurae, which he perceived as obstacles to free expression, and adopted a flexible quantitative meter from women's songs. In later years, this meter became popular in literature, with the name Apparao gave to it in the first line of the poem: *mutyāla-sarālu*, string of pearls.

The Comet (5)

"Mutyālasaramulu," (1910) *Gurajāḍa Racanalu: Kavitala Samputam* (Vijayawada: 1984)

Light of the Day: the sun

koil: a spring bird, similar to the cukoo

The comet is called *dhūma-ketuvu*, tail of smoke. In popular mythology Ketuvu (Dragon's Tail) is an enemy of the moon and in literature a woman's face is compared to the moon. Apparao plays on the word *ketuvu* connecting it to the planet and uses the literary convention to tease the woman for turning her moon-face away from the comet.

An interesting story tells of the origin of Ketuvu and explains its enmity to the moon. Demons and gods churned the ocean of milk to find the essence of life (*amrta*). When the *amrta* was found, the gods, who did not want the demons to have any share in it, prayed to God Vishnu to help them. Vishnu came as Mohini, the temptress of the world. The demons, who were taken by her charms, agreed to let her serve the *amrta*. Mohini made the gods and demons sit in two different rows and began to serve them. Keeping the demons under her spell, she gave all the *amrta* to the gods so that there was nothing left by the time she came to the end of the row. One suspicious demon disguised himself as a god and sat in the row of gods. When Mohini realized that she had served *amrta* to a demon, she immediately hit him with her (i.e. Vishnu's) discus. The demon's head and body were severed, but he could not die because he had already swallowed a few drops of *amrta*. The head became the planet Ketuvu and his body, the planet Rahu— and since then, the two planets began to swallow the sun and the moon. That is why lunar and solar eclipses occur.

Gold (27)

"Kāsulu," (1910) ibid.

꩜ ISMAIL (b. 1928)

A very independent and refreshingly quiet voice in modern Telugu poetry, Ismail worked as a lecturer of philosophy in Kakinada, East Godavari district. While most of the Telugu poets of his time were busy in literary-political movements, controversies, and state sponsored academies of literature, Ismail stayed aloof and wrote his poetry un-mindful of its immediate reception. Ismail is perhaps the only poet in Telugu who successfully made words in his poems totally silent. His poems speak to us free from the phonetic barrier, quietly and directly.

The Buried Poem (19)
  "Padya Samādhi,"(1983) *Ismāyil Kavitalu* (Kakinada, 1989)

Donkeys in Anantapur (190)
  "Anantapuramlo Gāḍidalu," (1977) ibid.
  "Donkeys in Anantapur" is one of his very few political poems. It received attention when the connection between the title of the poem and the conference of Marxist-Maoist Revolutionary Poets, which was holding its sessions in Anantapur at that time, was noticed.

Poetry (20)
  "Kavitvam," (1979) ibid.

Seen from an Island in Godavari (87)
  "Dhaniyāla Tippa," (1983) ibid.

A Suggestion (65)
  "Sūcana," (1984) ibid.

Van Gogh's Ear (59)
  "Van Go Cĕvi " (1980) ibid.

The Wall (218)
  "Goḍa," (1977) ibid.

You (50)
  "Nuvu," (1982) ibid.

∽ JASHUVA (1895–1971)
Born in an outcaste community of leather workers, Gurram Jashuva wrote poetry energetically expressive of the conditions of the outcasts. He used conventional metrical verses and wrote in a style respected by the literary establishment, but his themes and images were sharply

critical of the upper castes. He taught elementary school and later did a number of odd jobs including one as a traveling commentator of silent movies. He received the attention and appreciation of a number of major poets and writers of his time. Social reformer Viresalingam, influential poet Chellapilla Venkata Sastri, and noted novelist Chilaka-marti Lakshmi Narasimham supported him with admiration. Recognized as the voice of the depressed castes, Jashuva received public acclaim and literary honors as well. His most famous work is *Gabbilam,* a long poem in two parts. Modeled after Kalidāsa's famous Sanskrit poem, *Meghadūta* (The Cloud Messenger), which depicts a message sent by an exiled lover to his beloved wife, Jashuva' s poem describes a message sent by a poor untouchable man to the great god in Banares. In Kalidāsa's poem the messenger is the cloud, while in Jashuva's poem the messenger is the bat.

The Bat Messenger (214)

Selected verses from *Gabbilam* (Gunturu, 1941; Vijayawada: Jashuva Foundation, Benz Circle, 1996)

The selection here is an adaptation from the early part of the original, rather than a close translation.

Thanjavur: in southern India, the capital of the seventeenth-century Nāyaka kingdom ruled by famous kings who patronized Telugu poets

Four hooded snake: refers to the Hindu social order of four classes—Brāhmana, Ksatriya, Vaiśya, and Śūdra

karma theory: a religious theory that explains that a person's present life is the consequence of what he or she did in a previous life. If one is born an untouchable in this life, it is because the person did something bad in a previous life.

I Was One of Them (213)

"Bahudésa-mata-mahā-praisattu talayūca ... ," ibid, 38.

The first ten lines of the poem describe famous Indians of recent history. They are: Vivekananda, who represented Hinduism at the Conference of World Religions in Chicago in 1893; Mahatma Gandhi, who defied the British empire using handspun cloth as a symbol of protest; Sarvepalli Radhakrishnan, who was elevated to the chair of philosophy at Oxford University, England; Rabindranath Tagore, who won the Nobel Prize for Literature in 1912; and Jagadish Chandra Bose, who demonstrated that plants feel pain and pleasure. In the last lines of the verse the poet speaks of himself as an untouchable who was excluded from Hindu society. As is well-known, the four-varna system of Hindu society treats the untouchables as the fifth and outcaste community, beyond the pale of society.

∾ KALOJI (1914–2002)

A poet who wrote biting satire in bitter anger, Kaloji Narayana Rao represents the people of Telangana. He stood with courage and spoke against police brutalities and other abuses of power both during the rule of the Nizam of Hyderabad and, later, the Andhra state government. Kaloji is rightly called the people's poet. He lived a simple, unassuming life and refused to bow to power or wealth. His life was totally occupied in speaking for his people, so that he has had no time to be a poet in the professional sense of the word, participating in literary circles and promoting his poetic career.

Born in Karanataka, Kaloji lived all his life in Warrangal. Trained as a lawyer, he never really practiced law, but played a prominent role in social and political movements in Telangana. When he read his poems, Kaloji cried and moved his listeners to tears. His poems are at their best when read aloud, but fall rather flat on the silent printed page. Problems of translating the oral quality of these poems severely restricted my choices in representing this important poet.

We Should Remember (137)
"Kātesi Tirālĕ," *Na Godāva* (Secunderabad: Desoddharaka Granthamala, 1953)

∾ KAVIKONDALA VENKATARAO (1898–1964)

A poet with an unusually individual voice, Kavikondala Venkatarao, unlike many other poets of the Bhāvakavitvam period was sensuous, ironic, and provocatively original in his depiction of life. His images and diction shatter normalcy and demand attention. He wrote poems in meters he had invented himself, four of which are included in *Vaitā-likulu,* the anthology of the Bhāvakavitvam period. He wrote a number of stories and songs, which were also very different from the routine style of his contemporaries. Critics of his time mistakenly called him the Wordsworth of Andhra, in the usual colonial eagerness to equate every Telugu writer with a famous English writer. His work is still largely unexamined by literary critics.

A Letter (55)

"Vārta," *Vaitāḷikulu*

Mail in the early decades of the century was delivered to villages not connected by railway train by a runner who carried a spear with bells.

Workers in Love (187)

"Kūliy'annala Kutukamu," ibid.

Laborers in Andhra sing erotic songs as they work.

Coral on heavy breasts, heartthrob at the sound of feet, love at first sight, and *waiting for the beloved by the bush*: all of these refer to actual words in songs workers sing

You on My Mind (49)

"Ĕnduku?" ibid.

ᐁ KHADAR MOHIUDDIN (b. 1955)

A well-known Muslim poet, Khadar Mohiuddin cuts through the current fashions of literary style and directly presents the collective experience of Indian Muslims. Translated here is his most widely read poem from his 1991 volume, *Puṭṭu Macca.*

Birthmark (225)

"Puṭṭu Macca," *Puṭṭu Macca* (Hyderabad: Kavitvam Pracuranalu, 1991)

Krishna District: a district in the state of Andhra Pradesh

1947: the year India gained its political independence from Britain, which also marks a major outbreak of communal violence between Hindus and Muslims

The throne of three lions: India's official seal, the Ashokan capitol with its four lions facing four directions, only three of which are visible from any one side

Uncut Bhārat: *Akhaṇḍa Bhārat*, India as it was before partition, which included what is now Pakistan; it is the agenda of the right-wing Hindu religious groups of India to undo partition and merge the area under Pakistan into India

Magic touch: the original refers to a foot ointment (*pādalepana*) given by a magical healer, *siddha*, to Pravara, a Brahmin who flies to the Himalayas by its power; the story is told in a sixteenth century Telugu poem, *Svārociṣamanusambhavamu*, written by Allasāni Pĕddanna, a court poet of King Krishnadevarāya

evil clown-antagonist: Muslim characters are represented as clownish villains in Indian films and plays.

I can't revere your great poet: reference to the great Telugu poet Sri Sri who coined a new word *kasāyibu*, which combined *kasāyi* (butcher, cruel person) and *sāyibu* (a colloquial word for Muslim)

people's singer: reference to Suddala Hanumantu, a revolutionary singer of the Telangana peasant revolution, who sang songs exhorting people to kill the Nizam of Hyderabad, a Muslim ruler against whom the peasants revolted; however, he exhorted the people to kill Muslims without distinguishing the Nizam from the poor Muslims of the state, many of whom fought in the revolution

Article 370: an article in India's Constitution that accords a special status to Kashmir, where Muslims are a majority; the personal law refers to the religious law that governs Muslim marriages and divorces; Hindu religious groups demand abolition of personal law and advocate a secular uniform civil code for all Indians

∽ KONDEPUDI NIRMALA (b. 1957)

A well-known poet who writes with a gentle sense of confidence and quiet courage, Kondepudi Nirmala is one of the earliest women writers who wrote on feminist themes. Her writing continues to reflect contemporary political and social issues. The poems selected here do not, however, represent her better-known work, which is more activist in tone and political in content. She works as a journalist and lives in Hyderabad.

Birds Love the Net (204)

"Valani Premince Piṭṭala Jābita," (1994) *Badhā-śapta-nadi* (Hyderabad, 1994)

⌒ MACHIRAJU SAVITHRI (b. 1951)

An engineer by profession, Machiraju Savithri was born in Andhra Pradesh and moved to North America in 1960. She has lived in the United States and Canada, and kept up her interest in Telugu literature by reading and writing. Her short stories and poems have been published in various magazines in Andhra Pradesh and the United States and one of her novels was serialized in a Telugu magazine. She currently lives in California.

Black and White (236)

"Tĕlupu Nalupulu," (1984) *Macchu Tunakalu: Kavita-sankalanam*, ed. Pemmaraju Venugopala Rao (New York: Telugu Association of North America, 1993)

This poem, which could have come only from her experience in North America, is a unique contribution to Telugu literature. It presents a racial theme that Telugu literature produced in the mainland has never depicted. The poem draws attention to the semantic transformation in modern Telugu of words indicating the color of Hindu gods. The Telugu word *nalla* and the Sanskrit word *nila* are synonyms—both words indicate a range of dark colors from blacks to blues. But in its modern Telugu usage, the Sanskrit word has shifted to mean blue, and the Telugu word exclusively indicates black. Hindu gods such as Rāma and Krishna are no more perceived as black; they are blue. The poem marks a critical recognition of the fact that this shift in color of the god's skin demonstrates that Telugu people prefer to consider themselves light-skinned. It makes a striking and uncomfortable statement that the Telugu people are subconsciously racist. The poem is slightly abridged in translation.

Krishna: dark deity of Hindus

Pārvati, Draupadi: Hindu goddesses, also dark in color

the temptress of the world: Jaganmohini, Vishnu's incarnation as a beautiful woman; see the myth on page 250

∾ MADDURI NAGESHBABU (b. 1964)

A Dalit poet who published extensively, Madduri Nageshbabu's poems are published in five collections: *Velivāḍa* (1995), *Raccabaṇḍa* (1996), *Loya* (1997), *Ūru: Vāḍa* (with Rani Sivasasnkar, 1997), and *Mīr'evuṭlu?* (1998). He writes in a voice of anger, protest, and total defiance of upper-caste dominance. Most of his poems are responses to specific incidents of violence against untouchables.

What Do I Want? (234)

"Em Kāvāli?" *Mīr'evuṭlu?* (Narasaraopeta, 1998)

stolen by Manu: refers to the classical Brahminic code attributed to Manu, the *Mānava dharma-śāstra,* which justifies the hierarchical caste order of Hindu society with the untouchables at the lowest end

∾ MAHE JABEEN (b. 1961)

Born in Nellore into a Telugu Muslim family, Mahe Jabeen is trained as a social scientist. She runs an institute of social service in Hyderabad. Her poetry marks a new and refreshing confluence of love and revolution, feminine desire and social protest. Her images of youth and energy brought to Telugu poetry a world of sensuous hope and a revolutionary vitality at a time when routine revolutionary vocabulary desensitized it to all human feelings of tenderness and love. Her volume of poetry *Ākuralu Kālam* (1997), was received with acclaim by readers of poetry all over Andhra.

An Act of Caution (57)

"Mundujāgratta Carya," (1993) *Ākurālu Kālam* (Hyderabad, 1997)

fire as our witness: Hindu marriages are conducted in front of fire, with the god of fire as witness

Author's Consent (61)

"Atani Samakṣamlo," (1992) ibid.

Fall (209)

"Ākurālu Kālam," (1992) ibid.

Ideal Wife (207)

"Ŏka Paccani Jīvitam," (1995) ibid.

masjid: mosque

mandir: Hindu Temple

Ayodhya: According to the ancient Sanskrit epic text the *Rāmāyaṇa*, Ayodhya is the name of the legendary city where the Hindu god Rāma is born. The present day Ayodhya is a city in the Uttar Pradesh state of northern India, where the Mogul King Babur built a famous mosque called the Babri mosque in the sixteenth century. The Hindu Nationalist Bharatiya Janata party (BJP) claimed that the Muslim King Babur built his mosque on the site of Rāma's birth by destroying an existing temple. The BJP made rebuilding Rāma's temple a political issue and made it a part of its election platform. In 1997, a determined Hindu group led by BJP activists destroyed the Babri mosque. Ever since, the Mosque/Temple has been a violently debated issue in Indian politics.

tāḷi: the traditional string with two round gold pendants tied by the husband at the time of the wedding, which a Hindu woman wears on her neck as long as her husband is alive

bŏṭṭu: a dot on the forehead, worn by modern Hindu women as a part of their makeup; ritually, it is an indication that the woman is not a widow

Live Walls (144)

"Batikina Goḍalu," (1991) ibid.

Physical Geography (206)

"Naisargika Svarūpam," (1993) ibid.

Relationships (66)

"Sannihita-sambandham," (1997) ibid.

∽ NAGNAMUNI (b. 1939)

When a tidal wave killed thousands of villagers on November 19, 1977, Nagnamuni wrote the long poem *Kŏyya Gurram* (Wooden Horse). The poet's response to the disaster received considerable attention and was discussed for several months among literary circles. Nagnamuni is the name the poet adopted when he and five other poets formed a group called Digambara Kavulu (Naked Poets), which wrote poetry rejecting all middle-class standards of decency and used obscene insults against social hypocrisy and political corruption. For an analysis of the poem and its background, see Velcheru Narayana Rao, "A Storm and a Poem: Nagnamuni's *Wooden Horse* Revisited after Twenty Years," *Indian Literature* 196 (March–April, 2000): 166–77. Nagnamuni's birth name is Manepalli Hrishi Kesavarao.

Wooden Horse (159)

Kŏyya gurram (Hyderabad: 1980; 1999)

It is for the good of the world: a famous line from the *Āndhra-sabda-cintamani*, a grammar of Telugu written in Sanskrit, attributed to Nannayya (eleventh century) and considered the first grammar for the language

gets stuck between the thighs of young heroines / in erotic poems: a reference to the explicitly erotic descriptions in premodern Telugu poetry

and in the stories of ointments you rub on your feet / to make yourself fly: Pĕddanna, the court poet of the sixteenth century king Krishnadevaraya, narrates in his *Svārociṣamanusambhavamu,* the story of Pravara, who is given a foot ointment, which instantaneously flies him to the Himalayas

~ NANDURI SUBBARAO (1895–1957)

Subbarao was famous and controversial for writing love songs, called *Yĕṅki Pāṭalu*, in a low-caste dialect. His characters are Yĕṅki, a farm girl, and Nāyuḍu, a young peasant who is her *bāva,* her mother's brother's son, or her cross cousin, who according to Telugu custom she is ideally expected to marry. The two characters became the talk of the town in the Bhāvakavitvam days. Pundits and leaders of upper-caste taste, however, rejected his work as vulgar. The spelling of the name Yĕṅki itself was unacceptable to them; it was a low-caste distortion of the upper-caste Vĕṅki. Low castes in the coastal districts typically dropped the initial "v," a marker of upper-caste speech. The songs were controversial—not so much because of their theme, but because of their dialect. Very soon the language caught the fancy of middle-class young men and women, for its very difference from upper-caste speech. Yĕṅki songs became popular, prominent singers sang them and they were also broadcast on the radio. It was easier for the middle class to fantasize about love by identifying themselves with a low-caste, and therefore distanced, couple. Gradually the Pundits began to accept them, and Pancagnula Adinarayana Sastri, a well-known scholar, even went to the extent of finding in them the supreme aesthetic experience of rasa. Soon imitators followed, and among them, songs called *Baṅgāri Māma Pāṭalu* by Konakalla Venkata Ratnam are noteworthy.

Blow Out the Lamp (41)
  "Dīpam," *Vaitāḷikulu*

He Didn't Come Back (40)
  "Ānāṭi Nāvoḍu," ibid.

Is This All! (47)
  "Sandramu," *Mahodayamu: Ādhunika Khaṇḍikā Samuccayamu*

My Love (45)
  "Jaṇṭa Nā Yĕṅki," *Vaitāḷikulu*

You in My Dream (43)
  "Kalalona Nā Yĕṅki," ibid.

∿ NIRASANA KAVULU

A group of four poets Abburi Gopala Krishna (b. 1937), Attaluri Narasimha Rao (b. 1946), Bhairavayya (b. 1942), and Kottapalli Satya Srimannarayana (b. 1947) anonymously wrote under the collective name Nirasana Kavulu (Protesting Poets). They wrote in protest of the Revolutionary Writers Association (Virasam), which adamantly insisted that every poet write poetry for the cause of Marxist revolution and condemned all those who did not do so. A small volume of poetry published in 1983 by this group made an impact for its biting satire.

Among the four, Gopala Krishna and Narasimha Rao teach at Andhra University, Waltair. Bhairavayya, whose birth name is Mulukutla Manmohan Sahay, was one of the Digambara Poets (his "Raped Poem" written during his Digambara phase is included in this anthology). He lives in Visakhapatnam and does odd jobs. Srimannarayana was trained as an engineer. He published a volume of his own poems, *Vĕluturu-piṭṭalu* (Birds of Light), and now works as an electrical engineer for the state government.

Forces of Production (197)
  "Praṇaya-gīti," *Nirasana* (Visakhapatnam, 1983)

Me? (194)
  "Nenu," ibid.

∽ PATHABHI (b. 1919)
One of the most interesting poets of the Bhāvakavitvam period. With his *Phiḍelu Rāgala Ḍajan* (A Dozen Tunes on the Fiddle) he declared the end of the romantic period and the death of Bhāvakavitvam. Educated in Santiniketan under the great poet Rabindranath Tagore, he rebelled against Tagorian sentiments. He wrote in a deliberately "non-poetic" diction and ridiculed the asexual love of Bhāvakavitvam poets. Intentionally shocking and carefully crafted to read neither like poetry nor like prose, Pathabhi's prose poems broke the back of metrical verse that had lost its meaning in a wilderness of mechanically measured lines. Pathabhi wrote very little, but his *Phiḍelu Rāgala Ḍajan* made him instantaneously famous. At the height of his prominence as a modern poet in the 1950s, he declared he was not a poet anymore and went into the restaurant business. He wrote puns and cryptic verses afterward, but did not want to be involved in the literary scene seriously. In later years Pathabhi produced art movies, including the well-known *Samskāra*.

Moon in China Bazaar (192)
  "Jābilli," *Phiḍelu Rāgala Ḍazan* (1939); reprinted in *Pathābhi Pel-china Phiraṅgulu* (Collected Works of Pathabhi) (Hyderabad: Pathabhi Amrtotsava Samiti, 1994)
  China Bazaar is in the downtown section of Madras.

Sita (185)
   "Sīta," ibid.

∽ RAYAPROLU SUBBARAO (1892–1984)
A student of Rabindranath Tagore at Visvabharati University, Santini-ketan, Rayaprolu is credited with beginning Bhāvakavitvam in Telugu. He is known for his *Ramyālokamu,* a work on literary theory in verse, which served as a manifesto for his contemporaries. Rejecting the bold eroticism of classical poetry, Rayaprolu propounded a theory of beauty untouched by sexuality. Using the classical term *sṛṅgāra,* he called his concept *amalina śṛṅgāra* (pure love, or love untarnished). Most of Rayaprolu's work is now limited to literary-historical interest, but some of his work still reads beautifully.

Chained (30)
   "Sankĕḷḷu," *Vaitāḷikulu*

Waiting (31)
   "Virahavīthi," ibid.

∽ REVATI DEVI (1951–1981)
Very little is known of this extraordinary young woman who commit-ted suicide in 1981, when she was barely thirty. Her only book of poems, *Śilālolita,* is a posthumous publication. At the time of her death, she was completing her Ph.D on Jean Paul Sartre at Sri Venkateswara University, Tirupati. Several poems in *Śilālolita* contain italicized lines, with no explanation as to why they are italicized. In her preface she refers to improvements made to her poems by a close friend, but iden-tifies neither the friend nor the improvements.

A Birth (201)
   "Jananam," *Śilā-lolita* (Tirupati, 1981)

Cold Meat (70)
   "Hṛcchiti," ibid.

Distance (63)
   "Dūram," ibid.

The original has the following lines at the end, which I did not include in my translation: "Between him who is far away / and me—a distance / that not even air can enter. / This distance is indivisible."

Going out of Town (51)
"Ū'reḍutunnānu," ibid.

Invocation (54)
"Āvāhana," ibid.

No Break (158)
"Nirvirāmam," ibid.

This Night (157)
"Ī Rātri," ibid.

This World, Poor Thing (191)
"Pāpam Ī Lokam," ibid.

∾ SATISH CHANDAR (b. 1958)
Mailabattula Satish Chandar was born into an outcaste community. He works as a journalist. His poems that depict the experience of untouchables make a significant contribution to modern poetry. One of his poems included here, "A Child Is Born," was written after a clash between the upper-caste people and the untouchables in Tsundur, Andhra Pradesh, during which a number of untouchables were brutally murdered.

A Birth Postponed
"Ōka Jananam Vāyidā," *Pancama-vedam* (Hyderabad, 1995)
rejected by razors, scissors: barbers, who belong to a higher caste, did not cut the hair of the untouchables
protect them from molten lead: ancient Sanskrit law books prohibited lower castes and women from hearing the Vedic chants; if they dared hear the chants, however, the punishment prescribed was that molten lead be poured into their ears
low caste recruits: refers to the employees recruited under the regulations of affirmative action

A Child Is Born (219)

"Śiśuvu neḍu lecĕnu," ibid.

∾ SHAJAHANA (b. 1974)

A new voice in Telugu poetry, Md. Shajahana Begum has published some ten poems and is included in *Jaljalā* (1998), the recent anthology of Muslim poems.

Qaus-e Qazah (202)

"Qaus-e Qahajah," (1997) *Jaljalā* (Nallagonda: 1998)

∾ SISHTLA UMA-MAHESWARA RAO (1909?–1953?)

An extraordinary voice in modern Telugu poetry, Sishtla Uma-maheswara Rao was educated at Banaras Hindu University where he did his M.A. in English literature. His contemporaries report that he lived a chaotic life and was personally obnoxious. They say that he drank a lot, talked loudly, believed he was making a revolution in Telugu poetry, and insisted they listen to his poems. According to Sri Sri, Sishtla was gay, but we have no evidence of this. There is no reliable record of his date of birth or death. He served in the military, went to jail in the freedom struggle, returned to Madras to do odd jobs or live off friends, and died under "suspicious" circumstances, about which no one gives any details. He was tall and hefty, strong enough to lift and throw people of average build, such as Sri Sri, with whom he often quarreled. Sri Sri, in his autobiography, describes a heated argument between himself and Sishtla regarding who among them is the leader of modern poetry. During this argument, Sishtla lifts Sri Sri, swings him, declares an imaginary haystack nearby, and throws him in it. The story acquired different variants and people began to say that Sishtla really tried to throw Sri Sri into a burning haystack. Sishtla wrote under several pen names with weird spellings. He did not keep copies of his work. He printed exactly 128 copies of his poetry volume *Vishnu-dhanuvu* (1938) because, "there are just that many people in Andhra who would understand my poetry." In the same year, he published another volume of his poems, *Navami-ciluka*. These two volumes are now collected in *Vishnu-dhanuvu, Navami-Ciluka* (Hyderabad: Sri Sri Smaraka Samstha, 1998.)

Memories (114)

"Nāperu Līla," *Kalpana, Ādhunika Kavitā-sampuṭi,* eds. Anisetti Subbarao et al. (Vijayawada, 1953)

One of the few early modern poems that capture the female voice, "Memories" is composed in multiple tones that haunt the reader. The beginning of the poem reads like prose, like a factual narrative, and then the tone changes from reminiscing to day-dreaming to delirium before it ends in despair, calling on god Rāma. The rhythm changes accordingly, from a song, to a lullaby, to a scream. The original includes the names of village goddesses, Ĕnnĕmma and Kottĕmma, and their brother Poturāju. Ĕnnĕmma is a dangerous goddess that eats new born babies, and Kottĕmma is her younger sister.

Ahalya: Sage Gautama's wife, whose story is told in the Rāmāyaṇa; Gautama discovers her affair with Indra, the king of gods, curses her and turns her into a rock; Ahalya regains her original form when Rāma's feet touch the rock

୶ SIVA REDDY (b. 1943)

Arguably the most effective poetic voice in Hyderabad, Siva Reddy stands out as a revolutionary poet, though he is not a member of any revolutionary literary organization as such. He has published eight volumes of poetry and received the Sahitya Akademi (National Literary Academy) award for poetry in 1991. Siva Reddy is known for his public poem, a poem that is best read aloud. Most of his poems speak in a rhetorical voice and carry their listeners into an activist mode. A friend of many young poets, Siva Reddy plays a prominent role in the literary circle of Hyderabad.

Generations (177)

"Taram mārinā . . . ," (1975) *Śivāreḍḍi Kavita* (Hyderabad, 1991)

We Write (142)

"Mem Rāstū Vuṇṭām," (1982) ibid.

∾ SIVUDU (b. 1931)

Sivudu is of the several names adopted by Kambham Gnana Satyamurti, a revolutionary activist who wrote poems while he was involved with the Marxist-Maoist revolutionary group. Satyamurti was active in the formation of the Revolutionary Writers' Association (Virasam). Later he left the organization to work for the Dalit movement. The poem included here was written when Dr. Chaganti Bhaskara Rao, a revolutionary activist, was killed by the police. Satyamurti is now popularly known by another of his pen names: Siva Sagar. Satyamurti's attempt to adopt the rhythms of village songs for his poems succeeds flawlessly in the poem included here.

Warrior, Bhaskar! (139)
"Narudo, Bhāskarudā," *Jhanjha: Geya- saṅkalanam* (Hyderabad: Viplava Racayitala Sangham, 1970)

∾ Smile (b. 1946)

Mohammed Ismail adopted this name to distinguish himself from the older poet, Mohammed Ismail, who is also included in this anthology. Friends in literary circles distinguish the younger Ismail by his famous short story called *Khāḷi Sīsālu* (Empty Bottles) and call him Sīsāla Ismail (Bottles Ismail). He worked as an officer in the department of commercial taxes and is now retired. He has written very little but everything he wrote left a mark on modern Telugu literature.

Nothing Happened (68)
"Ramiñcesukunnām gadā . . . ," (1991) *Khaḷi Sīsālu* (Hyderabad: 1995)

∾ SRIRANGAM NARAYANA BABU (1906–1962)

Known as one of the leaders of the modernist movement in Telugu poetry, Srirangam Narayana Babu was well-known for two decades before 1950. Born in Vizianagaram in northern Andhra, he spent his later life in Madras. He tried to create a newness in his imagery, and left an expressive space between his images, which can be bridged only by the reader's active imagination. He loved music and wrote several poems on musical themes. He worked closely with Sri Sri, and the two poets shared many creative moments. In the late forties and after, Narayana Babu was almost totally overlooked under the glare of Sri Sri's prominence in the Marxist-inspired Abhyudayakavitvam movement. Narayana Babu did not care to keep his manuscripts or collect his work published in various journals. Not until Arudra published Narayna Babu's poems for the first time in 1972 (*Rudhirajyoti*), was his work available in one place, and even then, few people read him. Narayana Babu's personal life was tragic. His wife went insane, and he lived a lonely life, moving from place to place, doing odd jobs.

A Blade of Grass (151)

"Gaḍḍi Parakani," (1939) *Rudhirajyoti* (Vijayawada: Navodaya Publishers, 1972)

One of the earliest poems in Telugu supporting the untouchables. The blade of grass in this poem is an obvious symbol of the lower castes who have for centuries accepted their subordination and are now rebelling against their opressors.

dūrvāṅkura: Sanskrit for a blade of grass

that sharp fellow: Darbha grass (*Poa cymosuroides*), has a sharp edge. Gods and anti-gods churned the essence of life from the ocean of milk, but Vishnu cheated the anti-gods of their share. The snakes, who did not get their share either, licked the sharp grass where the pot stood. Their tongues were split into two, but they stayed young, only shedding their skin as it got old.

We decorate your finger: Brahmins put a ring of darbha grass on their finger during ancestral rites, when they offer food to their dead fathers.

punished the demon: An anti-god in the form of a crow lusted after Sita during her stay in the forest. He pecked at her breast as she lay on her husband Rāma's lap. Rāma sent a blade of grass to kill the crow. The blade chased the crow all over the world, until he repented and surrendered. The crow was allowed to live, but only after he gave one of his eyes to the blade of grass.

Let's Go to Hell (183)

"Preyasito Narākāniki," (1959) ibid.

Hell here is the Hindu *narakam*.

ritualists: Brahmins who perform Vedic rituals to please Indra, the king of heaven

romantics: poets who sang of platonic love during the Bhāvakavitvam period

Vaitaraṇi: The name of the river between this world and heaven, it is described as a river of pus and blood, impassable for any except persons who have earned merit during their time on earth. Relatives offer a cow as a gift to Brahmins at death rituals so that the cow will help the deceased person cross the *Vaitaraṇi*. The dead person, it is believed, holds on to the tail of the gifted cow, which then swims across the river to heaven.

burning oil: one of the details of the torture chamber in hell, sinners are fried in it

Chitragupta: Assistant to Yama, the god of death, he keeps accounts of people's deeds on earth and reports the balance of good deeds and bad deeds of the dead person so the soul may be properly judged.

buffalo of the god of death: Yama uses a male-buffalo as his vehicle.

Sex Everywhere (188)

"Leṇḍoyi Ruṣhulu," ibid.

This poem ridicules the Brahmin Pundits who advocated a life of religious purity, and control of desire.

roll up the earth: the kind of things sages in mythology are said to have done

The Sound of Silence (93)

"Mauna-śaṅkham," ibid.

This poem is a tour de force of surrealist poetry in Telugu. The poem uses the names of his close relative and friend Sri Sri and the romantic poet Krishna Sastri, and refers to the contemporary literary conflict between Krishna Sastri and Sri Sri. (The poems of Sri Sri and Krishna Sastri may be found elsewhere in this anthology, and a discussion of their work is in the After-Essay.) Irreverent references to gods and goddesses of the Hindu religion and the use of sexual images and objectionable language were controversial when this poem was circulated.

Blue Hills: the Nilgiri Hills in Tamilnadu, south India, a summer resort for the rich and an underdeveloped region of tribal people

when Rukmiṇi was longing for love: A popular mythological story from the Bhāgavata-purāṇa, in which Rukmiṇi, who is in love with Krishna, elopes with him on the day of her wedding to another man— a match fixed for her by her elder brother. Parents in Andhra encouraged their unmarried daughters to read this story with devotion to Krishna so they can find proper husbands. There is also a teasing humor implied in this and the next line. Here, Narayana Babu hints at one of his poet friends, Rukmininatha Sastri, who wanted to get married but was having a hard time finding a bride. Similarly, in the following line, "family" brings to mind another writer friend, Kutumba Rao. In Telugu, Kutumba means family. (Thanks to Avantsa Somasundar for providing this reading.)

snake Sesha: In Hindu mythology, Sesha is the snake that bears the burden of the earth and also serves as the bed on which Vishnu sleeps in the middle of the milky ocean.

Indra: king of the gods

Vajra: Indra's weapon, usually translated as the thunderbolt. According to one story, Indra used *Vajra* to cut off the wings of all the mountains when they used to fly freely and settle wherever they pleased, causing disastrous destruction of life.

gaṇḍa-bheruṇḍa: a huge mythological bird, often figures as a motif in temple sculpture

goddess of poetry: Sarasvati

Silver Mountain: the abode of Śiva and Pārvati

Pārvati: wife of Śiva

I left out a line here because it is unintelligible.

volksleid: a folk song

the merchant of German words: The original reads: *"jarman sāhitya komati"*; Somasundar suggests that this refers to Dr. V. N. Sarma, a scholar of German literature in Madras who was reportedly rather tight-fisted in his dealings with friends. *Komaṭis*, the merchant caste, are stereotyped in Andhra as being stingy.

mutyāla-saram: a meter popularized by Gurajada Apparao (see page 249)

sprung rhythm: A forcefully accentual verse rhythm in which a stressed syllable is followed by an irregular number of unstressed or slack syllables to form a foot equal to that of the other feet in the line. Coined by Gerard Manley Hopkins (1844–1889).

Dali: Salvador Dali (1904–1989), surrealist painter

Man Ray: (1890–1976), surrealist photographer

Upanishads: religious and philosophical texts of Hinduism

so'ham: An utterance in the nondualist religious traditions of Hinduism, which means: "I am the ultimate reality."

the first father: Ka'syapa Prajāpati, the first father who created the gods and anti-gods

the sage who brought the river from the sky: Bhagīratha, the sage who, undaunted by obstacles and repeated failure, brought Gaṅga, the river in the sky to flow on the earth

ᗩ SRI SRI (1910–1983)

Recognized as a great poet in Telugu, Sri Sri, whose complete name is Srirangam Srinivasarao, wrote extensively and influenced generations of poets. Often compared to Pablo Neruda and Mayakovski, Sri Sri led two Marxist literary movements in Telugu, the Abhyudayakavitvam (Progressive poetry) movement in the 1940s and the Viplavakavitvam (Revolutionary poetry) movement in the 1970s. His greatest strength is his mastery of the phono-esthetics of the language, which give his poems a powerful singability. In that sense, he is a public poet, a poet who moves large groups of listeners *en masse*. By the very same token, most of his poems, regarded by many of his admirers as the most moving and powerful, defy translation. Most of the effect of the poem is in its phonetic texture, deprived of which the poem is reduced into shallow political rhetoric. Sri Sri's greatest work is *Mahāprasthānam* (The Great Journey), which revolutionized Telugu poetry.

An Announcement (149)

"Jaya-bheri," (1933) *Mahāprasthānam Modalaina Gītālu* (Machilipatnam: Nalini Kumar, 1950; Vijayawada: Visalaandhra Publishing House, 1954)

A Bitter Poem (155)

"Cedu pata," (1937) ibid.

Call of Poetry (14)

"Kavitā O Kavitā," (1937?) ibid.

Myth of Myself (100)

"Svakīya purāṇam, (1980) *Maroprasthānam,* ed. Chelasani Prasad (Hyderabad: Virasam Publications, 1989)

Kodavatiganti: Kodavtiganti Kutumbarao (1909–1980) was a prominent short story writer and critic; active in the Marxist literary movements, Kodavatiganti was a close friend of Sri Sri's.

Really? (105)

"Nijaṅgāne?" (1941?) *Mahāprasthānam Modalaina Gītālu*

Some People Laugh / Some People Cry (91)

"Koyi has rahā hai, Koyi ro rahā hai," *Srī Srī Sahityam,* vol 2, part 1, ed. K. V. Ramanareddy (Madras: 1970)

The Vedantist (112)

"Mithyā-vādi," (1937?) *Mahāprasthānam Modalaina Gītālu*

The Wheels of Jagannatha (133)

"Jagannāthuni Ratha-cakrālu," (1940) ibid.

These selections may also be found in *Sri Sri Sāhitya Sarvasvam* (Complete Works of Sri Sri) 20 vols., ed. Chalasani Prasad (Visakhapatnam: Virasam Publications, 1986–1999).

༄ TENNETI SURI (1911–1958)

Suri did not write much poetry, but the poem included here made a mark for its rhythm and directness and is remembered decades after it was written. He worked most of his life for the daily newspaper *Āndhra Patrika* and the literary monthly *Bhārati*. He is known for his novels, *Jengis Khan* and *Rěṇḍu Mahā-nagarālu,* a translation of Charles Dickens's *A Tale of Two Cities,* and especially for his satirical play *Sāhitya-samavākāram,* in which contemporary literature is presented as a carnival. A very quiet and unobtrusive person in life, Suri had a sharp and critical eye for literature. In his play he did not hesitate to make devastating remarks against some of the most influential literary personalities of his time.

Here Comes God (86)

"Kilu Gurram," *Mahodayam* (Tenneru: Krishna District, 1959)

❧ TRIPURANENI SRINIVAS (1963–1996)

A young poet of promise and energy, Srinivas began writing poetry under the influence of Marxist revolutionary ideology. For some time he was closely associated with Virasam, the Revolutionary Writers Association, but moved away from it to write poetry in his own style. He worked on the editorial staff of *Āndhra Jyoti,* a daily newspaper in Vijayawada. In a short time, he rose to take full charge of its literary section. He then moved to Hyderabad as editor of *Āndhra Jyoti Weekly,* where he died in a motorcar accident.

During his short life he did a number of memorable things. He energized a number of young poets and created a taste for good poetry among readers. He started a small publishing house and published well-designed volumes of poetry. Titles published under this imprint are collector's items now. Srinivas's poems are published in two volumes: *Rahasyodyamam* (1989) and *Ho* (1987).

Chasing Memory (128)

"Veṇṭāḍutunna Jñāpakam," *Rahasyodyamam* (Hyderabad: Kavitvam Pracuranalu, 1989)

❧ VEGUNTA MOHANA PRASAD (b. 1942)

Mohana Prasad is probably the only poet in Telugu who writes poems that defy Telugu syntax. His early poems from his *Citi-Cinta* express a fragmented subjectivity and a broken universe. Resorting to the undertones of words, Mohana Prasad, who writes under a monosyllabic pen name Mo, is known for poems depicting a language that can not be spoken in any words, and a world that can only be silently groped at through words that have gone blind of sensibilities. Mo is a quietly disturbing poet who depicts the contemporary confusion of content, while his critics accuse him of losing contact with the external world and, perhaps, even with his readers.

Empty (126)
"Vĕlti," *Rahastantri* (Vijayawda, 1991)

First Blood (21)
"Rajasvala," (1973) ibid.

Hades (125)
"Lo-vĕlugulu," (1976) ibid.

Liberation (22)
"Vimukti," ibid.

Stupidity (127)
"Avivekam," (1987) ibid.

∿ Viswanatha Satyanarayana (1895–1976)
Despite controversy and contestation, Viswantha Satyanarayana stands out as the greatest Telugu poet in the twentieth century. He is prolific— he wrote epics, novels, poems, short stories, plays, and literary criticism. His work runs into thousands of pages and defies classification as modern or classical. Satyanarayana wrote in a classical style, vigorously defended Brahminic ideology, but powerfully depicted modern sensibilities. He wrote on contemporary issues but his critics complain that his style is hard even for the most erudite scholar of Telugu and Sanskrit to understand. Satyanarayana began writing in the 1920s in the mode of the Bhāvakavitvam. The first two poems chosen here are representative of his work from this period. The poems from *Śrī Krishna-saṅgītamu* belong to the later period when he wrote more like a classicist. Satyanarayana rejects the secular Krishna of the Bhāvakavitvam and creates an entirely religious and yet modern image of Krishna. The verses of *Śrī Krishna-saṅgītamu* are a tour de force; they read like prose, are meticulously metrical, and still have the complexity of a modern narrative.

The Beginning (10)
"Avatārika," (1932) *Srimad-rāmāyaṇa-klapavṛkṣamu, Bālakāṇḍamu* (Vijayawada, 1944; sixth edition, Vijayawada: Viswanatha Publications, 1992)

Verses translated here were selected from the first chapter of Satyanarayana's magnum opus *Rāmāyaṇa Kalpavṛikṣamu* (Rāmāyaṇa, the Wish-Giving Tree). Condemned by his tireless critics as a most dense, idiosyncratic, totally blemished and unintelligent work, and praised by his admirers as the greatest poem of the century, Satyanarayana's *Rāmāyaṇa* is an extraordinary modern poem written in a language relentlessly classical and yet brilliantly contemporary. Its demanding style replete with archaic words, long compounds, and erudite metrical verses makes it impossible for any one other than an old style scholar trained in classical texts to read it. Its refreshingly new sensibilities make it difficult for anyone other than a modernist to appreciate it.

Tirupati and Venkata Sastri: Two poets who wrote together in the early part of the twentieth century, Divakarla Tirupati Sastri and Chellapilla Venkata Sastri were famous with a collective name—Tirupati-Venkata-kavulu. Among them, Venkata Sastri, also referred to here as Venkana, was Satyanarayana's teacher. Legends about the twin poets and especially Venkata Sastri are told all over Andhra. Despite his energetic admiration for his teacher, Satyanarayana derived nothing from Venkata Sastri's smooth and easy-flowing style of versification, and set out on his own individual path. Clearly referring to this and perhaps also hinting a mild disapproval of this idiosyncratic individuality on the part of his student, Chellapilla Venkata Sastri said in one of his oral verses about Satyanarayana:

> No, he doesn't follow me,
> though he is my student.
> Nor does he follow any one of my fathers or grandfathers.
> His style is totally something else.
> But that is no reason not to accept him.
> He is beyond the ordinary.
> That's why this student of mine is called the king of poets,
> and that makes me very happy.

Nannayya: Recognized as the first poet in Telugu, Nannayya belongs to the eleventh century and wrote the first two and a half books of the Sanskrit epic the *Mahābhārata* in Telugu. Tikkana of the thirteenth century completed the remaining fifteen books of the epic while the missing half of the third book was written by a fourteenth-century poet Errapragada.

Kodali Anjaneyulu: A poet from the Bhāvakavitvam period, Kodali Anjaneyulu (1897–1982) is remembered for his lyrical poems included in *Vaitāḷikulu*. Soon, he moved away from lyrical poetry and entered the nationalist movement against the colonial British government. He and Viswanatha Satyanarayana wrote under a combined name Satya-Anjaneya poets. Their collaborative work, *Avatāra-parivartanamu* (Change of Incarnation), depicting the change of leadership of the freedom movement from Balagangadhara Tilak to Mohandas Gandhi, was confiscated by the British government. The whereabouts of the manuscript are not known. Anjaneyulu was imprisoned for four years for writing poetry against British rule. He wrote an autobiographical poem *Ajñāta Satyāgrahi* (An Unknown Freedom Fighter).

The Blind Beggar (74)

"Andha-bhikṣuvu," (1930) *Vaitāḷikulu*

Though included in *Vaitāḷikulu*, the anthology of Bhāvakavitvam poets, this poem shows in its syntax evidence of classicist tendencies in Satyanarayana's poetry.

Hundred for Rāma: A well-known collection of one hundred poems addressed to Rāma, the Hindu deity, written in the late seventeenth century by Kañcĕrla Gopanna (popularly known as Rāmadāsu) a tax collector (*tahsildar*) at Bhadrachalam under Abu'l-Hasan Tanashah [Tel. Tānīṣā] of Golconda. The tradition has it that he misappropriated money from the treasury to build the Rāma temple at Bhadrachalam and was imprisoned for this for twelve years; during these years he composed *Bhadrādri Rāmadāsu Kīrtanalu* (Songs for Lord Rāma of Bhadrādri), and a book of one hundred verses for Rāma of Bhadrādri (*Dasarahī Śatakamu*). Rāma himself, together with his brother Lakshmaṇa, went in disguise to the Sultan, paid him the cash that was missing (six lakhs of rupees) and had the poet released. The verses and the songs were popularly sung by devotees as well as mendicants and beggars.

Song of Krishna (80)

From *Śrī Krishna-saṅgītamu* (Vijayawada: V.S.N. and Sons, 1969)

The selections are from *Śrī Krishna-saṅgītamu* 25, 26, 34, 57 and 81.

Śūrpaṇakha: A demoness in the Rāmāyaṇa who falls in love with Rāma

while the latter was in the forest with his wife Sīta and brother Laksh-
maṇa. Rāma orders his brother to cut off Sūrpaṇakha's ears and nose
as punishment for her behavior.

Your Chariot (73)
   "Nīrathamu," (1927) *Vaitāḷikulu*

A HISTORICAL
AFTER–ESSAY

A recurring theme in the history of early-twentieth-century Telugu poetry is the rejection of the past and the celebration of the new. It was neither easy, nor realistically possible, to break away from a literary tradition of almost a thousand years; but that was what the modern poets thought they achieved in so many ways. Declaring the period immediately preceding British rule as the dark age in Telugu literature marks the self-legitimizing act of the new poets of the century. A historical amnesia erases their memory of an active movement of modernity that flourished during the sixteenth and seventeenth centuries during the rule of the Vijayanagara kings and the Nāyaka kings of Thanjavur and Madurai.[1] To review the unfolding of the saga of new modernity, we need to visit the literary scene of the eighteenth and nineteenth centuries, long devalued and neglected in Telugu literary history.

THE LITERARY SCENE IN THE
NINETEENTH CENTURY

Telugu literature in the eighteenth and nineteenth centuries presented a dynamic and innovative world of language practices.[2] In this world, the *kāvya* was the superior genre of poetry, which engaged the attention of the elite. This genre was predominantly erotic with ornate descriptions in a learned style intended for accomplished readers. Excellence in the genre was determined by the poet's ability to describe, to innovate, and to create a playful semantic universe with the skillful use of language. Genres such as *purāṇas* and *māhātmyas* were primarily religious and carried mythological narratives with a didactic content. Historical writing took the form of *caritras*, written in both prose and verse. Other genres of poetry such as *padams, kīrtanas,* or *jāvalis* were favored for their lyricism rather than for their scholarly erudition. Another genre was the *Śataka,* a series of about a hundred poems addressed to a deity, preferred by poets for writing social criticism or to express their personal moods. Prose was extensively used for books on the sciences from medicine to mathematics, from astronomy to archery. Taste in poetry was the hallmark of culture, and literate people quoted verses from memory in conversations and at assemblies. These verses, called *cāṭu* verses, related literary anecdotes about poets and their patrons, courtesans and their relationship to the poets, and expressed reflections on the nature of literary language, the beauties of literary texts. The *cāṭu* world created an arena of intertextual relationships involving a linkage between texts and their past and present contexts.[3] In addition to this vast body of literature, a variety of unwritten texts—what we now call oral literature—circulated extensively among people, both scholarly and nonscholarly, upper- and lower-caste, men and women alike. Texts had built-in hierarchies indicated by their use of language, style, and meter. But all classes of texts—high and low, written and unwritten—interacted in the common oral world they shared.

This literary world encountered an alien world in the shape of the modern. Modernity and its consonant virtues began to rub against the world of traditional texts as the power/knowledge nexus of these two worlds differed widely.

MODERN?

With the end of the Maratha wars during the early nineteenth century, the English East India Company consolidated its power over much of peninsular India, where Telugu had been the language of court and transregional communication. The change in patronage structures, from the earlier Nāyaka style courts to a presidency administration, although seemingly discrete, brought forth a fundamental cultural break. Increasingly founded upon ideas of science and industrial capitalism, the East India Company rule and later the Crown rule of India displayed their new power and status dressed as exclusive products of a superior race, nation, and civilization.[4] The most important aspect of this new supe-riority was the English language, which through the administrative practices of the British Raj reproduced its symbolic power over the Indian cultural universe. English literature, once considered unworthy to be taught in the universities in England, became the embodiment of civilization for the non-Christian world of the colony.[5] The new civ-ilizational ethics of the Raj elicited a variety of responses from Indian scholars. While Europe experienced a complex interplay between the secular and the Christian worlds, colonial India had to contend with Christian morality reformulated in the garb of a civilizational morality. If in Europe the secular and the Christian world views evolved within the same symbolic and cultural field, thereby mutually influencing each other, in colonial India the world of the secular Raj was implicitly Christian in its moral outlook.

Premodern Sanskrit and Telugu poetry, both courtly and religious, were replete with descriptions of women and lovemaking. The erotics of Sṛṅgāra rasa, an important literary mode in Telugu and Sanskrit for centuries, became, for the first time in history, a moral problem. Prominent intellectuals stated, and social activists generally agreed, that Hindu culture was depraved and lacked moral discipline.[6] The war of morals was most central to the construction of the Telugu literary canon for the century. Filtered through the values of Victorian moral-ity, everything that was erotic in Indian literature looked obscene and immoral. Texts of the past now became the targets of a new moral regime. This is best understood when we see the story of one such text, *Bilhaṇīyamu* (a late-eighteenth-century Telugu reworking of a Sanskrit poem, attributed to the eleventh century poet Bilhaṇa), which was ex-tensively read in Telugu literary circles of the late nineteenth and early twentieth centuries.[7]

Bilhaṇa, a Sanskrit scholar and a handsome young man, is appointed by the king to teach his daughter, beautiful Yāmini. The king, con-cerned that Yāmini might fall in love with the handsome Bilhaṇa, orders a curtain to be placed between them during their classes. Yāmini has vowed not to set eyes on a blind man, and Bilhaṇa has vowed that he will not gaze at a leper. These vows serve the king in justifying the curtain: he tells Yāmini that Bilhaṇa is blind, and Bilhaṇa that Yāmini is leprous. On a night with a full moon Yāmini hears Bilhaṇa singing beautiful verses describing the moon. Wondering how a blind Bilhaṇa could describe the moon, she lifts the curtain. She finds that he is not blind, and he sees that she is not a leper. Irresistible to each other, they end up making love.

Yāmini's father, the king, condemns Bilhaṇa to be beheaded. As he is being dragged to the place of execution, Bilhaṇa continues composing verses recalling his love and sends one beautiful verse after another to the king in the hope of gaining forgiveness. The king finally forgives him and offers Yāmini in marriage to Bilhaṇa.

Moralistic concerns generated by this text at the turn of the century may be attributed to two obvious reasons. First, the transgression of a student-teacher relationship was a problem. Second, the descriptions in the text were extremely erotic. As was indicated before, colonial high morality of the nineteenth and early twentieth century found the erotic descriptions to be an example of the debased nature of Indian society.

As vocal critics of the "debased" Hindu tradition, Kandukuri Viresalingam, followed later by Cattamanchi Ramalinga Reddy, found in *Bilhanīyamu* an exemplary means to work out their arguments.[8] Viresalingam condemned the book as immoral and unfit to be read, and Reddy rewrote the poem cleaning up its sexuality. In Reddy's *NavaYāmini* (New Yāmini), Bilhaṇa falls in love with Yāmini only to be told by her that his desire is immoral. She argues that, as a teacher, Bilhaṇa is akin to a father and friend and admonishes him for giving in to his weaknesses. Bilhaṇa, grateful to his student for showing the way, goes on to lead a virtuous life. Reddy took care to describe the beauty of Yāmini in clean asexual vocabulary, describing only her inner virtues.

Reddy, in his *Kavitva-tattva-vicāramu*, went on to condemn some two hundred years of Telugu literature as decadent for its erotic themes.[9] While accepting the epic retellings of the *Mahābhārata* and the *Rāmāyana*, and some major works of Telugu *kāvya* written during the age of Krishnadevaraya, Reddy summarily rejected the bulk of classical

Telugu literature as distasteful because of its erotic indulgence. Backed by important officials in the colonial economy of education, both Viresalingam's and Reddy's views on literature held immense disciplinary power over literati of the colonial towns and cities. A new civilization was on the rise with science, history, and morality as the symbols of its superiority. Scrutinized under the new standards, the existing literary culture with its three pillars—*purāṇa, kāvya,* and *cāṭu*—was found to be seriously lacking. *Purāṇa* was superstitious, *kāvya* was immoral, and *cāṭu* was unhistorical.

Complex Modernities under Zamindari Patronage

During the late nineteenth and early twentieth century, literary and cultural patronage centered around small kings. These royal patrons were mainly tax farmers for the British rulers. In the absence of real power, these little kings tried to make up for the lack in the world of literature and culture. Following the style of the royal patrons of the past centuries, they supported scholars and poets within their limited resources. But their world was shrinking as more and more urban centers were opening to English education and the benefits of modern learning. Some of the zamindars themselves began to patronize new learning by supporting English educational institutions, while others entertained Sanskrit and Telugu alone. If the colonial cities and institutions received a direct impact of the social reforms advocated by Viresalingam, the Zamindari centers gave rise to a more nuanced response to science, history, and morality while trying to keep their respect for the indigenous practices. Two poets, Chellapilla Venkata Sastri and Gurajada Apparao represent two different expressions of this development.

Chellapilla Venkata Sastri (1870–1950) did not receive an English education. Born into a scholarly Brahmin family, he was trained like the Pundits of the earlier generations, by one-man-institutions of great teachers in *vyākaraṇa* (grammar) and *kāvya* (poetry), in both Sanskrit and Telugu. Drawing on such solid learning, he composed poetry in Telugu in the traditions set forth by classical poets. Never having worked for an English patron or a government institution, he did not imbibe the insecurities that result from accepting colonial cultural superiority. Apparao, on the other hand, was trained in English educational institutions; he had a bachelor of arts degree from the Maharajah's College, Vizianagaram. Well-read in Sanskrit, old Telugu texts, and English, he had a broader understanding of the massive changes happening on the world scene. Having come from a lineage of Niyogi Brahmin families who served premodern kings as ministers and political strategists, Apparao was sensitive to the changes in the nature and style of power. Venkata Sastri, on the other hand, came from a family of Dravida Brahmin Pundits who were Sanskrit scholars, poets and ritual specialists not directly involved in the politics of the court.

Corresponding to the variation in their respective educational and cultural backgrounds, Venkata Sastri and Apparao strove towards distinctly different goals. Venkata Sastri tried to establish for Telugu the literary glory that it had enjoyed until the end of the eighteenth century, whereas Apparao tried to create in Telugu a literature suitable for a modern world, which was just coming into existence. It is in this context that twentieth-century Telugu poetry begins.

Venkata Sastri made it his mission to attract the new English-educated middle-class gentry to Telugu poetry. He teamed up with his friend Tirupati Sastri and developed a joint style of performance. The two of them would improvise on demand for one hundred people, each of whom would ask for a poem on any topic, or a solution in verse to a riddle, or a poem conforming to preset restrictions (such as using only certain given words). Even more startling was their ability to remember all the poems they had orally composed and recite them on the spot without any lapse of memory. In their joint versification, one would compose the first line of a verse and the other would follow with the second line; both of them would then recite the entire poem at the end. These dramatic skills of spontaneous versification and phenomenal memory made the pair enormously popular among educated people; in turn, their fame imparted a respectable stature for Telugu poetry. Influenced by the twin poets, who were known as Tirupati-Venkata-kavulu, many younger poets teamed up in pairs and wrote verses together. Dozens of young men became poets under their charismatic influence. The popularity of their poetry was not limited to literate people alone. Verses from their plays on the *Mahābhārata* theme, which were staged all over Andhra, were memorized and recited even by nonliterate people in villages.

Venkata Sastri and Tirupati Sastri generated jealousies as well. Their opponents in the field of poetry were not few, either. Fierce literary disputes between them and their adversaries kept every one on both sides active, even to the point of litigation. These quarrels were often conducted in verse, later published in journals and as separate books. Venkata Sastri was a formidable opponent and wielded his verse with great skill in repartee.

A major development of Venkata Sastri and Tirupati Sastri's literary performances and their arguments was that the public space in Andhra became energized. Their poetry served as the arena in which questions, from the grammatical acceptability of certain new words to the new ideas of language and politics, were discussed and debated in every town wherever educated men gathered. The witty poems they composed in response to the questions and challenges they faced in their poetry performances and in the literary duels they fought with their opponents were instantly circulated among educated people, and were quoted in conversations all over Andhra.[10]

But the fame of two great Telugu poets was not enough to improve the status of Telugu scholars and poets in the colonial academy, which was clearly in favor of English. Venkata Sastri wrote, deploring their situation:

> They now read proofs at printing shops
> just to stay alive,
> or teach Telugu to white Huns,
> expound religion in the houses
> of those grocers who give them credit.
> Phenomenal scholars have been humbled.
> Times have changed.[11]

For Apparao, on the other hand, this would not have been a matter of much consequence. For him, both Sanskrit and Telugu were out of touch with reality, which was changing in the face of modernization and English education. Together with his patron, Ananda Gajapati, the king of Vizianagaram in northern Andhra, he recognized the need to accept the changes English education had brought and the opportunities that came with it. He envisioned future events with great insight and developed a far-reaching literary agenda for himself. His program was to clear the path so that a modern Telugu prose could emerge, and to modernize Telugu sensibilities with a new kind of poetry—a sort of cultural revolution, to create the basis for the emergence of a new class of people who would have both the cultural confidence to assimilate alien influences without being defensive, and who would also possess the intellectual strength to retain what was valuable in their past. His agenda was vast—in a way much larger than he could have completed in the short span of his life. He also showed, both in his play *Kanyā-śulkam* and his poem "The Comet," that the social reformist ideas that were being promoted by Viresalingam were shallow and misguided and would not really bring about a desirable difference in the life of the people—a message still not fully realized by his admirers. He rewrote themes of violation—popular in mythology and legend—not to give sermons on moral behavior, but to reinterpret them to reflect new civilizational values. Thus we find in Apparao's work the story of Sārangadhara, where the young wife of an old man desires the love of her stepson; the tale of Kanyaka, where a ruling king tries to molest a merchant's daughter; and as was mentioned before, the story of Bilhaṇa, where a young princess and her teacher fall in love. He wrote the first poem in Telugu on male bonding, borrowing the theme of Damon and Pythias from Roman mythology.

Apparao's poem "Gold," about romantic love between a man and a woman, a theme that would soon set the trend, merits a close look. The theme hardly seems earthshaking for us today, but in early-twentieth-century Andhra, for a husband to say that he loves his wife and that he wants to offer his heart to her, was simply revolutionary. To the wife in that culture, the husband's words are strange, and totally meaningless. Here, the husband addresses his wife,

I brought you a heart full of love
like a precious diamond.
Take it.

A confused wife—who is trained to accept the man her parents married her to even before she reached puberty, to serve him at his command, and to receive ornaments as gifts from him—does not quite understand the image of a heart full of love like a precious diamond. She asks a very practical question: How does she wear such a diamond? Needless to say, the rest of what he proclaims is even more confusing to her, especially when he says:

Husband is an old word.
I am your friend,
poor without your love.
But if I have it, I'm
richer than the king of gods.

Reading the poem as a woman listening to her speaking husband, we can see that the agency to love rests with the man; the woman remains a recipient, not one who reciprocates, much less initiates love. Irrespective of the praise of her beauty, something a conventional wife is not used to hearing, and the platitude that follows—"You love and you are loved. / You give love to get love."—and also a confession that his life is dark without love, we can also see that the love he so proudly announces here is not mutual; it is his, and it is his life that is brightened by it. As a wife, she is perhaps inure to such one-sided statements. No wonder she feels cheated for not getting a real diamond. She makes her husband understand her feelings with her looks. Sheepishly the husband responds: "You think I tricked you with a poem / instead of giving a real gift?" and tries to justify himself with an embellishment of his earlier romantic drivel, "This poem is pure gold / when you lend your ears to it."

He innocently expects his wife to listen to it as he sings it—to accept it as an ornament on her ears, very different from the earrings she would love to wear. (In the original the ornament is a gold chain. Based on an untranslatable pun on *kaṇṭham*, the poem "becomes pure gold" in her voice/neck.)

Observing the structure of the poem, we see that it is not really a singable poem. It reads like prose, though technically it follows meter. It is not even a conversation. The husband does all the talking, with the confused wife giving her responses with her looks, or with an expressive silence.

The readers of the time were confused too. This simple poem looked like a bold celebration of love, but was too unadorned to be called a poem. The editors of *Vaitāḷikulu*, the prestigious poetry anthology of the Bhāvakavitvam movement, which came a few years later, were equally confused, but could not reject the work of the first modern poet in Telugu. They edited out the first and the last parts of the poem, which sounded too prosaic, and included in the anthology a small middle section of the poem beginning with the line, "Love is everything" and ending with "Without love / life is dark." For them this was a good enough love poem. Clearly, Apparao had a different agenda: he intended his poem to quietly expose the shallowness of the rhetoric of love in the context of arranged marriages.

Such is the tricky nature of Apparao's poems. The surface meaning is quietly subverted by the silences of the poem or by oblique counterstatements, often made by a woman in response to the ebullience in the man's voice. This is revolution enough—in ideas, in words, in meter, and in the very mode in which the poem appears, unadorned, without the fireworks of Sanskrit compounds, so disarmingly simple that no one even notices this is a poem.

Let us take a look at Apparao's poem "The Comet." The poem is structured in two halves, a husband talking to his wife in the first half and the wife responding to him in the second half. With the dominating presence of the husband's lecture, the poem looks like a scientific statement on the nature of comets and a revolutionary defense of English education. It sounds very hopeful with its new images of the comet as heralding reform; it makes prophetic statements about the abolition of caste and a happy-ever-after life free from the ignorance of the small minds of the past. The poem even risks being preachy to make an elaborate point. The entire dream is built around a short visit to the city and conversations with a few reformers who organized an all-caste meal, as a first step to reform.

The second half of the poem is the wife's reaction. The husband's long lecture on reform and the rosy picture he has painted have no impact on her. She is not half as excited as he is at these prospects. Rather, she knows that the entire enterprise is shallow. The new egalitarian society her husband is talking about is not going to emerge out of a common meal. She knows that only marriages across castes break the steel frame of caste society. In any case, English education is meant to give young men a passport to lucrative jobs, so they will be the next rulers of the country, after the British. The angry remarks of the wife, uttered as if they were words of rebuke rather than a well-thought-out critique of her husband's position, actually serve as a clearly articulated counterstatement revealing the false assumptions of her naive husband's lecture. The poem, which looks like a strong statement in favor of social reformist action and modernist ideas, is, in reality, a critique of such shallow positions.

Apparao, however, was not influential enough during his lifetime to turn the intellectuals or the poets toward his understanding of modernity. His life was too short, his literary output too meager, and his message too subtle to be understood by his contemporaries. In the absence of a nuanced modernism, which he envisioned, a different and less complex role was played by Rayaprolu Subbarao and Devulapalli Krishna Sastri in bringing about a modernity that has had a lasting impact on Telugu life.

Making a Middle Class, a Region, and a Nation
Love, rather than sexual desire; friendship rather than kinship; rebellion against the Pundits rather than respect for authority—these became the hallmarks of a new period of poetry that held sway over the poetic imagination. In a society where an individual has always been identified with reference to caste, family, and gender, the new poetry, known as Bhāvakavitvam (poetry of feeling), speaks of a new person without

the social distinction markers prevalent in earlier writings. This new poetry followed the accepted conventions of language and meter but rebelled against the presentation of social and personal relations in traditional poetry. Centered on love themes, the lovers of the Bhāva-kavitvam world do not have a caste, class, or religion. In this literary universe, the pronouns "I" and "You," stripped of their social markers, suffuse the *mise en scene* of the emerging nation. The poets of Bhāva-kavitvam spoke of a golden age of the nation through the reimagining of historical and religious themes now "discovered" by epigraphists and historians. In contrast to the new reality of industrialism, this poetry imagined an idyllic village community, nurtured in a natural landscape. The low-caste, low-income farmers of villages are now endowed with a middle-class style of love and romance, unaffected by hunger or poverty. In this universal middle class, unblemished by overt sexuality, the Telugu language, history, and culture reign supreme—often in conscious opposition to Tamil nationalism, but proudly presenting the glory of India's classical past. The new poets believed they were the harbingers of a dawn of freedom after a troubling night of decadence.

Love, which depicts personal feelings of friendship, was the ideal of these poets. A man may love and adore a woman, sacrifice himself for her, but she remains bodiless. If earlier poetry left no part of woman's body untouched—including her breasts, thighs, and pubic hair—the new poets preferred instead to concentrate on her heart and her feelings; if they ever approached the physical body, the best that they could do was to describe her curly hair and her dark eyes. Bhāvakavitvam celebrated *prema,* love for her, rather than *moha,* desire for her.

Until then, the worlds of nonsexual love and sexual love were very clearly separated, with distinct terminology for each of these domains. *Prema* was nonsexual love, which a person has for one's mother, father, brothers, or sisters. Sexual love was *moha* or *kāma,* somewhat charged words, with their own dangerous consequences. The sexual and non-sexual worlds never mingled; their respective semantic boundaries were never violated. Now, for the first time, *prema* was used to encompass a sexual relationship as well. The result was far-reaching, and the resistance to the mixing of domains was fierce.

The idea of love was enchanting to the younger generation. The new poets were charismatic, the words they used to convey the feelings of a man for a woman were delicate, and their lyrical style was captivating. Bhāvakavitvam spread like a gentle breeze carrying a maddening fragrance.

Rayaprolu Subbarao (1892–1984), the leader of this new school of poetry, was an admirer of C. R. Reddy but did not follow Reddy's rejection of classical Sanskrit texts.[12] But he believed, like Reddy, that erotic descriptions in poetry were not good taste. Rayaprolu still called his love *sṛṅgāra*, borrowing the Sanskrit term for the erotic; but he qualified it by the adjective *a-malina* (unblemished, clean).

Another important shift brought forth by the poets of Bhāvakavit-vam was the extension of devotion to god into the secular realm of the nation. A person could now be devoted to the country (*de'sa-bhakti*)—complete with its history, territory, and language—as one would be devoted to a deity. The symbolic world of personal feelings was now redeployed so as to create an emotional bond with the country. The new poets wrote patriotic poetry extolling Mother India, and Mother Telugu. The land, which in premodern literary texts had been routinely described as the "wife" of the king, now becomes the mother—who should be protected by all her children. King Krishnadevaraya, who is now identified as a Telugu king, and other such heroes of the past are children of the Telugu motherland. These poems stirred the emotion of pride among Telugus, in conscious opposition to the Tamils who, at that time, dominated the south. The glorious past history of the nation—including the Telugu people's own history, diligently constructed by the nationalist historians—came to occupy the attention of the Telugu middle class.

If Rayaprolu was the forerunner of modern lyrical poetry in Telugu and the leader of the Bhāvakavitvam movement, the greatest poet of this movement was Devulapalli Krishna Sastri (1897–1980). A master of the lyric and a charismatic personality, Krishna Sastri influenced a generation of new poets, and more significant, created a whole new community of readers whom he trained in the ways of appreciating the new poetry. He traveled all over Andhra giving poetry recitations and talks. He brought a message of freedom and declared that a poet should write as his heart dictated, rejecting all the controls of the Pundits, their rules of language and poetics. Inspiration, rather than education; spontaneity, rather than control; passion, rather than scholarly training; and the heart, rather than the head—these were the hallmarks of the new poet. Krishna Sastri lived the life of a free spirit. He did not accept any job in which he had to serve a boss or any patron to whom he had to write on command. Legends were told about his independent personality.[13] In his vision, even the great classical poets were good only because they, the best of them, wrote precisely like the new poets did—in a manner that was lyrical, original, free, and following the dictates of the heart.

Krishna Sastri's inimitable style—combining soft words in Telugu and Sanskrit, mellifluous consonants coupled with the rhythmic vowels—made the lines of his poems move like the gentle waves of a cool breeze. This is a style that transports the reader into a dreamy state of mind, somewhere at the boundary of reality. Other poets tried to write like him, but virtually no one succeeded; they even imitated his hairstyle, wore glasses just as he did, and adopted his loose *lālcī* and *dhovati*. Hundreds admired him; he was the personification of Bhāva-kavitvam. Making gentle fun of his imitators, he wrote in one of his light verses:

> Gold-rimmed glasses,
> long hair and fun—
> there's nothing the new poet lacks.
> He is strong in everything except poetry.
> God, what else is left to say?[14]

Krishna Sastri was the prophet of the new poets. He dedicated one of his books to the woman he loved—loved and failed, and whose name he did not reveal. He called her Ūrvaśi, after the mythological woman of the gods. His poetry celebrated failure in love, suffering, languishing, dark nights, loneliness, and exile. Nonsexual love between the sexes was the professed ideal of his movement, but society itself,

with its arranged marriages and endogamous conventions, was not
ready to allow any real openness between men and women. God
Krishna's love for his cowherd girls or other such mythological themes
could be rewritten, transforming them into themes of secular love;
but to mention the woman next door in your love lyrics could be dis-
astrous. Men and women rarely met in private. There was a strict
separation between them everywhere—in schools, temples, buses, and
trains. Women never went out alone, not even to their friends' houses.
In this atmosphere, love between men and women could only be writ-
ten under the cover of mythological themes or imagined as if it was
happening in a never-never land above the earth. As the following
poem by Vedula Satyanarayana Sastri suggests, the poet could sing of
his girlfriend:

> She is the goddess of peace in my heart,
> a delicate flower from the depths of hope,
> a love song from the dawn of life ...[15]

but he would never mention her name or give any indication of who
she might be.

What Krishna Sastri and his followers achieved was a revolution in
literary taste and a new subjectivity, creative freedom, and individual-
ism. The role of the Pundit and his Sanskrit books on poetics had
ended; the poet was now the sole master of his creation. He had no
fears; nothing embarrassed him, and he recognized no master. Basa-
varaju Apparao openly ridicules the old Pundits:

> No one can stop me today,
> no one can resist my hold.
> Every word I say
> is worth its weight in gold.
> Pundits will run away from here
> hitting their bald heads in fear.
> No one can stop me today.
> Whatever I speak is song.[16]

In standing up to the old establishment of Pundits, the new poets found strength by forming literary organizations representing modernity. Navya Sāhitya Pariṣattu (Assembly of New Poets), formed in 1936, was one of the prominent associations that worked to energize modern poets in the face of establishment scholars. Poets also edited journals dedicated to literary innovation and conducted conferences and literary readings. Poetry was their life, their passion—not just a vocation or a profession. Poets in Navya Sāhitya Pariṣattu included people who had a vision of the future of poetry and were willing to work with promising younger poets in order to promote and publish their work. The new poets themselves took the lead in creating an audience for their poetry by establishing new standards of literary criticism. They were boldly polemical and organized to face the attack of the old-style Pundits, who sought to demolish the new poetry. One such Pundit was Akkiraju Umakantam (1889–1942), a great scholar and a fierce adversary of the new poetry, who mercilessly attacked every one of the new poets in his scathing study *Netikālapu Kavitvamu* (Poetry These Days, 1928). His learning and his wit were both formidable, and his assault on Bhāvakavitvam became so popular that some of the poets he attacked became famous because of his criticism. Major newspapers and journals were actively involved in publishing literary disputes; often poets themselves edited literary sections of newspapers.

The impact of Bhāvakavitvam was clearly discernible in the way the new intellectual elite and the new middle class began to think and feel during the first decades of the century. Just a few decades earlier, words such as *ādhunika* (modern), *svatantra* (independent), and the first person singular *nenu* (I), were not very positive words in Telugu. *Ādhunika* meant something that is recent and untested, and therefore not respected as standard; *svatantra* implied a lack of respect for authority and tradition and when used in reference to women it meant wayward; the use of *nenu* to claim authorship of an idea or initiation of an action implied lack of humility. The major epistemological shift in Telugu culture created and sustained by Bhāvakavitvam had a more enduring impact on culture than the poetry itself.

Modernists: Telugu Enters the Wider World
The hungry thirties shook the complacency of Bhāvakavitvam. The stories of the Great Depression, the October Revolution, and socialist internationalism were not only the stories about the West, but were true to the colonies as well. Their combined effects were far-reaching and captivated young minds. For the poets of the modern movement, Bhāvakavitvam seemed too otherworldly. They rejected the imagined love of Bhāvakavitvam, in which external social reality did not exist and images of poverty and economic malaise never appeared. The modernists spoke of a new awareness of social reality that implied class-consciousness, albeit still in the familiar romantic modes of Bhāvakavitvam. They created a new language separating the rich from the poor, the oppressive past from the liberating future, and called for a revolution against the economic exploitation and political power of the rich. The idea of the international working class had overtaken the naive idea of the nation without distinctions. Freud came to the support of the modernists to discover the unconscious and the role of sexuality in poetry. Love itself became unrealistic in the face of the compelling reality of arranged marriages. Rayaprolu Subbarao's asexual love—*a-malina śṛṅgāra*—became a joke. The severe effects of the Great Depression on the economy left most educated young men unemployed and disheartened. The first major attack on the ideology of Bhāvakavitvam—specifically, on the twin ideals of asexual love and romantic freedom—was made in the 1930s by several poets, Srirangam Narayana Babu (1906–1962), Sishtla Uma-maheswara Rao (1909?–1953?), Pathabhi (b.1919), and Sri Sri (1910–1983). All these poets, except Pathabhi, were known in Bhāvakavitvam. But Pathabhi was a new entity. He was educated in Santiniketan under the great Rabindranath Tagore, and turned a rebel against Tagore's romantic, visionary style of poetry. In the introduction (written in English) to his *Phiḍelu Rāgāla Ḍajan* (A Dozen Tunes on Fiddle, 1939), a book that created a sensation in the literary world, Pathabhi wrote:

I had a surfeit of lyrical poetry of Gurudev Tagore in the romantic atmosphere of Santiniketan for nearly two years. I joined the Calcutta

University for my literature M.A. and took up residence in the dingy rooms in the lower Chitpur road in Calcutta. The din, the squalor and the human misery shocked me to the core. The mad commercial activity of the city and the loathsome brothels of the Chitpur road, where innocence is exploited by avarice, disturbed me greatly.... As I lay on my bed and looked through the window, I saw the full moon surreptitiously peering through the smoke-filled sky. All the thousand metaphors I had read in the Bhāvakavitvam, in the Prabandhams and in Tagore songs suddenly lost all their meaning.

Pathabhi, whose real name was Pattabhi Rama Reddy, changed the spelling of his first name, made it his pen name and published poems that sounded irreverent with their irregular spellings, rejection of meter, and disturbing images. He summarily dismissed sweet poetic words like *venněla* (moonlight), *malayānilamu* (cool breeze), and *mallě puvvulu* (jasmine flowers), which the Bhāvakavitvam had popularized. Pathabhi's words were deliberately crude, his phrases were unprecedented in their rejection of smooth combinations of sounds, and were clearly meant to shock his prudish audience with openly sexual descriptions. The literary establishment was predictably outraged and called this ultra-modern poet (*ati-navya-kavi*) crude and offensive to good taste.

At about the same time, Sri Sri, Narayana Babu, and Sishtla were experimenting with different modernist influences derived from French and English poets. Vizianagaram and Visakhapatnam, the two northern Andhra coastal cities, were the centers of the modernist movement. Here are some lines from the surrealistic verses Sri Sri wrote during that time:

> Paint symbols of algebra
> on the body of a zebra.
> Dress him in a long dark coat, and ad-
> dress him: Sir, Dean of Letters.
> I'll tell you if you do not shout.
> This is what surrealism's all about.[17]

We'll break the laws of meter
and dismiss meaning to the equator.
We'll mate prose with verse in glee.
If they ask: "Damn it. What are you doing?"
We'll answer: "Sir, it is poetry we're creating."

Literary journals were receptive to modernism and the readers reacted to surrealism with a sense of curiosity and admiration. Freed from the controls of prescriptive grammars and Pundit-made lexicons, language was thrown open to innovative explorations. Sri Sri wrote: "even s-s-s-stammered words have a place in m-m-m-my poetry." Narayana Babu declared: "There's no theme, no word that is prohibited in our poetry—dirty clothes, bazaar streets, dogs, donkeys, stinking sewers, factory sirens, machine guns, poverty, sick old women—all of them— everything under the sky—are welcome here." Closely associated with this agenda of modernism was an acceptance of the philosophy of Karl Marx and a passion to change the world. Paraphrasing the eleventh thesis from Marx's *Theses on Feuerbach*, Narayana Babu wrote: "Philoso- phers have understood life and nature. We will change the world, life and even nature."

By the late 1920s socialist ideas were in the air. Indian students who were going to school in England and Ireland returned with ideas influ- enced by the 1917 revolution in Russia. In 1922–23 Unnava Lakshmi- narayana, who studied law in Ireland, wrote *Mālapalli,* a novel about the untouchables with Bolshevik ideas incorporated in it. The British government proscribed it, but had to lift the ban in 1928. Ever since Gandhi refused to negotiate with the British government to save the life of Bhagat Singh, an armed revolutionary who was on death row and was later hanged in 1931, young people, especially poets, began to be dissatisfied with Gandhian politics of nonviolence. Narayana Babu wrote a poem on Bhagat Singh. Krovvidi Lingaraju published his translation of Maxim Gorky's novel *Mother* in 1934, which was also banned by the government, but was vigorously read and secretly dis- cussed. The same year, the socialists who were in the Congress party formed the Congress Socialist party at the national level, and in

Andhra a Communist party was formed. A young Telugu poet, Bal-antrapu Nalinikantarao translated Eugene Pottier's "L'Internationale" into Telugu, which was sung at Communist party gatherings. Sri Sri wrote "Mahāprasthānam" (The Great Journey), which reads like a marching song with the rhythmic movement of strong Sanskritic clusters of consonants, liquids, and aspirates. Its dynamic movement and energetic phonetic patterns carry, at a breathless speed, its call for revolution, a call to the youth to march to the new world.[18] In 1935, Sri Sri, under the tutelage of Abburi Rāmakrishna Rao (1896–1979), who was the Librarian of Andhra University, read the "Manifesto of the Indian Progressive Writers, London" and was deeply influenced by it. By the time the collection of Sri Sri's poems *Mahāprasthānam Modalaina Gītālu* was first published in 1950, some ten years after they were compiled into a book-length manuscript, and some fifteen years after many of the pieces included in it were published in journals, Sri Sri was already recognized as a great poet.

Marxism and Literature: Poetry and the Party

As literary wings of the Communist parties of India, Marxist literary organizations served the political agendas of the party to which they were attached. If the party saw the industrial working class as the vanguard, so did the Marxist writers—regardless of the vastly nonindustrial nature of the society. When the party concentrated its activity on the hill tribes and landless peasants, the writers followed the lead. The saga of Marxist literary writing from the Abhyudaya movement to its later incarnation, Virasam (Revolutionary Writers Association), closely follows the high drama of the Communist parties and their changing political strategies. Poets who did not approve of this development either stayed outside the movements or left the organizations.

In 1943, years after Sri Sri's poems celebrating workers and the revolution impacted the literary field as part of a larger modernist movement, the Communists in Andhra began to take active interest in poets and writers. Under their guidance, Abhyudaya Racayitala Sangham (Progressive Writers' Association) was formed. Sri Sri joined the association, as did a number of other poets and writers. The association published a literary journal, *Abhyudaya* (Progress), which served as a forum for progressive writers and critics. Initially, the Abhyudaya movement included in its fold all shades of poets, from former Bhāvakavitvam poets to the later modernists, but it gradually developed into a serious literary-political organization. Modernist poetry, including what Sri Sri himself had written, was now clearly denounced as an irresponsible trend, reflecting a bourgeois anarchy. The multiple voices of Bhāvakavitvam poets were caricatured into a silly romantic tone. Sri Sri became the undisputed leader of progressive poetry, and as the poets in the organization began to write in support of the armed struggle organized by the Communist party in Telangana against the Nizam of Hyderabad, their poetry became strikingly political and revolutionary. The peasant revolt inspired a whole generation of poets. Noteworthy among them were Arudra and Avantsa Somasundar from the coastal area of Andhra, and Kaloji Narayana Rao and Dasaradhi from Telangana. Poetry became more and more politicized but gradually lost its impact as the Communist party suspended the revolt and the nation-state adopted many of the liberal features of the Communist party's agenda.

The 1968 tribal revolts and the sixtieth birthday celebrations of Sri Sri led to the renewed vitality of revolutionary poetry, resonating with Maoist influences. The revolutionaries joined hands with like-minded members of the now dormant Progressive Writers Association and formed a new organization, Viplava Racayitala Sangham (Revolutionary Writer's Association), popularly known as Virasam. Sri Sri was invited to be its president. The charismatic personality of Sri Sri and the appeal of the revolutionary message created massive enthusiasm for poetry among young readers, especially students. A group of young urban poets with modernist influences who called themselves Digambara Kavulu (Naked Poets) were attracted to the movement, and wrote along with hundreds of other young poets in support of a violent overthrow of the government. Ideas of a militant revolution, class war, and the annihilation of the feudal class were commonplace in every poem. The forest where the guerrillas were fighting became a literary symbol of progress. Journals dedicated to revolutionary literary organizations published hundreds of such poems, some of which were also released as separate volumes between red covers. In retrospect, few of these poems survived the immediate context in which they were written.

Thus, twice in a span of forty years, Marxist parties infused poets with their revolutionary message and harnessed their energies for writing for the people. Each time, the Marxist ideology interrupted what was shaping up to be a modernist movement in poetry. If the modernists were focused on the individual and the complexities of a fragmented consciousness, the Marxists led them to surrender their individual identity to the group and speak in the language of the masses. Phrases such as social consciousness and commitment, images of poets holding a gun in one hand and a pen in the other, were regularly paraded in poems and literary criticism. Battles were fought in the press between poets who argued for literary values and those who spoke for a revolutionary message.

Perhaps the most important and lasting contribution of the Marxist poets to literature is the song. During the height of the Marxist movement, song was the preferred mode of literature. Accessible to large audiences who were not completely print-oriented, song was a powerful medium to communicate a revolutionary message. Najar, during the Abhyudaya phase of the movement, and Gaddar, Vangapandu Prasadarao, and Subbarao Panigrahi during the Virasam phase, composed and sang songs to thousands who gathered to hear them.[19] In the 1970s, Gaddar was a force to be reckoned with. He inspired a number of young poets to write songs instead of free verse. Song was seen as a more powerful means of reaching people, and for a period of time it received literary attention. Gaddar came from a Telangana Dalit family, and Prasadarao from a Srikakulam peasant family. Each of them wrote in their low-caste dialect of Telugu. Major poets, including Sri Sri, followed their lead and wrote songs in a low-caste dialect. However, the songwriters have not been fully incorporated into the literary world with the literary-critical support such an enterprise needs. They are still seen as a separate class, valued only because they helped promote a specific political message, but not recognized as poets who produced works of literature.

Back to the Future: Return of the Traditional Repressed
By the early forties, the rejection of the past in literature was complete. The past, first attacked by the social reform of Kandukuri Viresalingam and later in literature by C. R. Reddy and his followers and then by the Bhāvakavitvam poets, was given a final blow by the heavy duty revolutionary vocabulary of the Marxist poets. Literary and textual standards that had held for several centuries were now almost totally demolished, to a point that a modern poet was embarrassed to invoke a premodern text in any context other than to condemn it as feudal.

Schools and colleges had a two-tier system of faculty: there were lecturers and professors, who had graduate degrees from colleges and universities, and Pundits, who were learned in the classical texts of Sanskrit and Telugu and had little or no knowledge of English. Lecturers and professors were paid higher salaries, while Pundits were poorly paid. They even dressed differently. Pundits wore traditional clothes, a *dhovati* and a buttoned coat, their heads clean-shaven with a tuft of hair, a *pilaka*, hanging behind and the religious *bŏṭṭu* marking their forehead. Lecturers and professors dressed in Western-style clothes, a shirt and slacks, with a jacket and tie and short hair. Even if the lecturers and professors occasionally wore a *dhovati*, they never shaved their heads or grew a *pilaka* and they taught almost every subject in English. Telugu was considered a second language, and was treated as optional. It was very clear to the students that English and subjects taught in English led them to a better future. Usually, students did not even attend their Telugu classes regularly, and they made fun of their Telugu Pundit, his *pilaka* and his manner of speech. They shouted and coughed and made animal noises in class. They badgered the Pundit with embarrassing questions about words and passages describing women and lovemaking in old Telugu texts. Care was taken not to prescribe texts that included explicitly erotic passages, but even relatively harmless selections had references to breasts, nipples, thighs, buttocks, and coitus, all of them old Telugu or Sanskrit words for which modern Telugu equivalents had to be provided. With young women in the same class, though on separate benches, the male students managed to embarrass them with mischievous questions addressed to the teacher. In these schools, the life of a Telugu Pundit was miserable. His general image was of a fossilized, unimaginative individual who somehow had instant access to all the old books he had memorized, but lacked the intelligence to study any modern subject. Students who had developed a taste for old Telugu and Sanskrit texts respected their Telugu teachers, and the more impressive and dominating personalities among the Pundits commanded a presence. In general, however, the status of the Telugu teacher was not high.

Marginalization of Sanskrit and old Telugu in the academy created a new intellectual who took pride in being uninformed of past academic traditions. Texts of grammar, philosophy, and poetics were now read, if at all, in their orientalist English translations. The modern intellectuals read English poets and Western philosophers, thought in English, and even wrote their personal letters, notes, diaries, and journals in English. Modern poets imagined a world of universal freedom and equality, in a casteless, classless society. In this brotherhood of man, the world would be one house, and all human beings would be one happy family. To the poets who wrote of freedom and equality, the old Telugu and Sanskrit texts appeared as an obstacle to a free society. A general opposition to the values of the past dominated the literary world.

At this juncture, one strong voice resisted the change—that of Viswanatha Satyanaryana. A student of Chellapilla Venkata Sastri, Satyanarayana (1895–1976) initially wrote some Bhāvakavitvam poetry, but soon he rejected it and went in the exact opposite direction by wholeheartedly accepting traditional literary styles. For him, the path of poetry was laid down by the eleventh century Nannayya, the first Telugu poet and author of the *Mahābhārata* in Telugu. In an atmosphere where it was fashionable to reject the old poetry and believe all great poetry began with Krishna Sastri, or with Sri Sri, depending on whether one was a Bhāvakavi or an Abhyudayakavi, the entry of Satyanarayana into the literary field, with a bold call for a return to the old values, meant war. In his writings Satyanarayana created a glorious traditional India. He supported everything the modernists considered problematic in the old Sanskrit books, including caste hierarchy, prepuberty marriages, and Brahmin superiority. The progressives condemned Satyanarayana as backward looking, while his admirers called him *Kavi-samrāṭ*, Emperor of Poets. Satyanarayana was prolific—he wrote about a hundred books—and he was versatile, composing in every genre of literature: poetry, song, novel, short story, play, satire, essay, and literary criticism. He had a phenomenal control of Sanskrit and classical Telugu; he could wield Telugu meters with a command superior even to the classical poets. A poem he wrote in one of his mythological plays for a king who brandishes his sword against the enemies of the Vedic sages came to represent Satyanarayana's rage against the enemies of tradition. The poem describes the Vedic sages in breathtaking Sanskrit words and declares war on their enemies:

ati-manobudhyahankṛtul'aupaniśadul'
ātta–gaṇḍūṣita–trayul'aurva–vahni-
garbhitāntah–tapaskulu ghanulu ṛśulak'
ĕvvaḍu virodhi tadvadhak'ĕttina yadi.[20]

They are beyond the mind, intellect or ego.
they speak the three Vedas with full-throated voices.
Fierce with the submarine fire in the depths of their inner self—
They are the seers, the wise men, the greats.
Anyone who dares to oppose them,
I'll kill him.

Satyanarayana's formidable scholarship was matched by his monumental imagination and creative energy. He took Telugu poetry to dizzying heights using mythological themes and writing in a classical style, but with compelling modern sensibilities. Boldly challenging those critics who argued against traditional values and traditional poetry, Satyanarayana took the less popular position, arguing that it was English education that made Telugu poets and intellectuals lose their heritage and their traditional excellence. Defying the fashionable modern position that themes like the *Rāmāyaṇa* were detrimental to the progress of society, he wrote a *Rāmāyaṇa* of his own, in six volumes, and called it *Rāmāyaṇa Kalpavṛkṣamu* (*Rāmāyaṇa*, the Wish-Giving Tree). In the preface to the book he asks and answers the question: Why *Rāmāyaṇa* again?

> If you ask, "Why yet another Rāmāyaṇa?"
> My answer is: In this world,
> everyone eats the same rice every day,
> but the taste of your life is your own.
> People make love, over and over, but only you
> know how it feels. I write about the same Rama
> everyone else has known, but my feelings of love
> are mine. Ninety percent of what makes a poem
> is the genius of the poet. Poets in India know
> that the way you tell the tale
> weighs a thousand times more
> than some facile, novel theme.

Satyanarayana's *Rāmāyaṇa* stands out as the greatest poem written in the twentieth century. The phenomena of his towering literary personality is inexplicable in a cultural and intellectual context in which the educated population had become thoroughly modernized under a colonial impulse and therefore was utterly unprepared to appreciate his creative genius. Satyanarayana was attacked for being hard to understand, for his archaic diction and his preference for difficult, arcane words that even the most erudite scholars could not follow. One of his admirers, Jalasutram Rukmininatha Sastri, even wrote a parody playfully imitating Satyanarayana's style:

> Torture us, please,
> impossible poet,
> with your exuberance of stunning words
> and delicious feeling slightly mixed
> with bitter dryness. We need jaws of stone
> to grind the elevated phrases you utter with ease
> as you tease us through your labyrinths,
> books cooked to the texture of rock.[21]

But Satyanarayana had his answer to his critics:

In the old days, if a text was demanding,
the reader felt it was *his* lack.
These days the poet is to blame.
Devious are the ways
of this dying age.[22]

For the next twenty-five years, the literary field was dominated by two personalities—Sri Sri and Viswanatha Satyanarayana—like two giants, commanding veneration among their respective followers. Rarely did one poet talk to the other, and critics on each side convinced their readers that what the other group was reading was rubbish. Simplistic and caricatured descriptions of both poets circulated freely. Modernists depicted Sri Sri as a forward-looking people's poet, an enemy of capitalists and imperialists. They represented Satyanarayana as retrograde, seeking the revival of feudal values linked to Brahmin superiority, an enemy of all progress and an anachronism in the twentieth century. On the other hand, the followers of Satyanarayana represented Sri Sri as a windbag and slogan maker, with no proper sense of what makes poetry, no sense of the aesthetic values of *rasa* or *dhvani* as defined in Sanskrit poetics.

Even in their appearance and lifestyles, Satyanarayana and Sri Sri were worlds apart. Satyanarayana wore the traditional *lālcī* and *dhovati* with a clean shaven head and a *pilaka*—the look of a traditional Pundit. Sri Sri, on the other hand, wore slacks and a short-sleeved shirt, more like a worker in a factory. Both came from orthodox Brahmin families, but Sri Sri smoked and drank, ate meat, and lived a thoroughly modern lifestyle, while Satyanarayana ate no meat, observed all the religious rules, and lived a strictly Brahmin lifestyle. In their public presentations, the poets looked more like two rivals at war than like two creative writers. They caricatured each other for the benefit of their supporters and delivered one-liners for laughs. It is almost as if they lived in two different countries, one alien to the other, and you needed a visa to cross the border. Such hard barriers prevented any critical evaluation of the varieties of modernity in both poets.

Satyanarayana's followers continue a somewhat unimaginative effort to keep the old literary styles, especially metrical composition, alive in the face of an avalanche of free verse. Critic G. V. Subrahmanyam identifies them as part of a continuing movement that unfolded after 1935. He calls it *Navya-sampradāya-vādam*, neoclassicism. The most noteworthy among them is Kovela Sampatkumaracharya, who wrote some very fine poems in his recent *Āmukta* (1999), a volume of poems in conventional meter on Goda Devi, the goddess who married the god Raṅganātha.

POST–MARXIST IDENTITIES

Feminists

Feminism, as an ideological opposition to a male-dominated world, initiated the end of the hold of orthodox Marxist ideas on poetry. Culminating in the publication of an anthology, *Nīlimeghālu* (Blue Clouds), in 1993, the movement began a decade earlier with several women independently writing poetry. Many were Marxist or leftist liberals who extended the practice of making social and political statements through poetry to their grievance against men and male oppression. Boldly stating, without much polemics, that a revolution does not in itself liberate women from male domination, women wrote defying the Marxist orthodoxy as well as conventional family authority. If there was a male writer they took inspiration from, it was the novelist Chelam (1894–1979), who had stood up for the sexual liberation of women and against the bondage of marriage. Writing during the height of Bhāvakavitvam and its message of asexual love, Chelam was far ahead of the times in advocating revolt against marriage as an institution. His writings passionately depicted the need for a society in which a woman can live intellectually, emotionally, and sexually free as an individual. His female characters live for their sexual desire uninhibited by middle-class fears and unmindful of the literary limits imposed by Bhāvakavitvam. He also played the role of a social activist when he wrote the first guide to women's physical health, *Strī* (Woman).

The fact that women wrote poetry was in itself nothing new to Telugu literature. There were women poets from as early as the thirteenth century, though many of them were not prominent. The heyday of women writers was the seventeenth and eighteenth centuries, when women such as Raṅgājamma and Muddu Paḷani rose to the position of court poets. That many of those poets were also courtesans became a matter of serious concern in the early decades of the twentieth century for the social reformers who were worried that such women could become role models. The social reform movement against the courtesans (the anti-nautch movement) stigmatized and eventually led to the dissolution of this community. This effectively put an end to the public presence of women. The same social reformers also encouraged women's education. A number of women from the upper castes wrote with the encouragement and support of their fathers, brothers, or husbands, but they did not enter the public world of poetry.

During the Bhāvakavitvam period women wrote in large numbers, too, though mostly in a somewhat pedestrian style following in the wake of the major male poets of the time. The literary magazines and literary anthologies carried poetry written by women, but no woman poet came into the open, giving public readings of her work or took an active role in the literary organizations of the time. It is ironic that a literary movement that made romantic love and the adoration of women the centerpiece of poetry did not recognize women poets for what they wrote. To be more exact, it did not pay attention to women poets except as tokens and did not even notice when a truly talented poet came along. Chavali Bangaramma (1897–1978) was the most impressive poet of the Bhāvakavitvam period. She published some twenty-five poems during her lifetime, and five of them were included in *Vaitāḷikulu*. But no one, literally no one, considered her a major poet. Some sixty years after she wrote, she remains to be discovered and recognized.

Outwardly, Bangaramma appears to belong to the literary atmosphere of the Bhāvakavitvam period. She wrote about the feelings of love and affection. She celebrated nature: hills, lakes, rivers, rain, clouds, moonlight, birds. She also wrote, like the other poets of the period, about the love between Krishna and Rādha, innocent little children, newly married brides, and God. But these themes only mask the originality of her poetry, which marks her as a poet unlike any of her contemporaries. A careful reading of her poems reveals not a romantic celebration of love, but a disturbing picture of pain and suffering of a lone woman.

Bangaramma uses a language that no other poet of her time came even close to trying. She uses the words women speak at home and infuses them with subtle undertones of rhythm and music. Male poets created a language of feeling by choosing only such words that sounded smooth and delicate, even as they borrowed heavily from high-sounding Sanskrit. The texture of poetry of this period created an atmosphere of dreamy romance. The major poets of this period, such as Krishna Sastri, were masters of this art. Bangaramma quietly rejects this style and adopts a language so personally her own: earthy, real, and subtly sensuous. Furthermore, poets of the Bhāvakavitvam period even tried to speak in a woman's voice when they wrote about women in love. But almost always their characters were faceless women, or faraway cowherd girls of Krishna stories (for example, see Devulapalli Krishna Sastri's poem "In Search of Krishna," included in this anthology). Women who wrote during this period imitated this well-established style in their works. Bangaramma was the very first poet in this century to bring a woman's voice into poetry and to create a language for it.

Bangaramma did not use conventional meters, which had been the mainstay of Telugu literature for almost a thousand years, and which the poets of Bhāvakavitvam continued to favor despite their rejection of most other conventions. Bangaramma wrote what is loosely called a song, but in fact she invented her own meters suitable to her diction and rhythm of speech. Literary criticism of this period was mostly dominated by a hybrid scholarly discourse derived from Sanskrit poetics and Western criticism. A few critics accorded a condescending approval to song, which was extended to Bangaramma's poetry as well.

Another significant feature of Bangaramma's poetry is that she rarely tells a story. Rather, she allows her images to speak and each one of her images shatters our expectations.

Let us take a closer look at her poem "Hibiscus on the Lake," perhaps the best she ever wrote. The poem is ostensibly about a lake and a hibiscus plant on its edge. The scenery is idyllic. The Telugu name for hibiscus, *mandāra*, is a delicate word, very feminine, very much like the flower itself with its brilliant red, luxurious petals. The erotic connotations of the flower are inescapable though subtle. The branches of the *mandāra* bush suggest a beautiful woman bending over the lake.

The first five lines of the poem give us the image of a placid lake. We are told that the flowering plant knows all about the beauty of the lake. In the fourth line the flowering plant sees her reflection in the water to put her forehead mark *(bŏṭṭu)* on. A woman who takes the time to look at her own face in the placid water to fix her *bŏṭṭu* suggests that she is conscious of her appearance and beauty. And for a *mandāra* plant, the red flower does look like a *bŏṭṭu* on the forehead.

Suddenly, without notice, the scene changes to one of horror. The person who is seeing all this—the speaker of the poem—faints from seeing the "beauty." The lake is no more placid. Now there are snakes crawling through the lake, and the sky itself trembles in fear and falls on the banks. Even the sun is frightened to see what has happened and hides behind the trees. We should note that the sun is often described in Indian poetry as *jagat-sākṣi*, witness to everything that happens on earth.

The images at one level may be taken to indicate only a disturbed surface of the lake. When the lake was placid, the reflections of the tall tree trunks were still. Now they look like crawling snakes. The quiet sky and the brilliant sun could be seen in the still water. Now the image is shattered. However, the crawling snakes, the fallen sky, and the frightened sun are not presented as similes, but as real events. The power of the events indicate more than a mere surface disturbance of the lake, such as when a stone is thrown into it. Something tragic has happened, whatever that may be. Was a woman raped in this secluded area? "She spread out her hair. / Her *bŏṭṭu* fell off" suggests some sort of violence. In the last part of the poem the lines, "The banks shed tears / and the shore was shaken" reinforce the tragedy. The flowering plant on the edge of the lake, which stands bent toward the water, remains the only witness. The description of the bent hibiscus plant here takes us back to the beginning of the poem, and returns us to the still picture of the serene lake with the hibiscus plant bending over it.

Throughout the poem the word beauty or its equivalent is repeated over and over but it changes its meaning at least three times. In its first two occurrences, it is the beauty of nature. In the third stanza, it gradually comes to mean something horrible and violent—the exact opposite of beauty. But in the last two stanzas the word recovers its surface meaning, but it now masks a horrible, unspoken tragedy. It turns into a word reflecting an ugly hypocrisy and a quiet cover-up. Does village life, so romantically sung about in many beautiful poems, hide unspoken horrors and tragedies? Is this what the poem is trying to express without openly speaking about it? The language of the poem is smooth, gentle and soft even as it describes horrible events. The poem ends with a seemingly simple statement, "The hibiscus talked to me." Only on reflection do we recognize that this line speaks of something hidden in the poem. The hibiscus is still bent, it couldn't stand up to (nor did it break under) the atrocities it witnessed.

Another poet of distinction is Revati Devi (1951–1981). Her presence was not known to the world until after her death and the posthumous publication of her poetry. Her book *Śilālolita,* however, did not receive much attention. Several years later, *Nīlimeghālu,* an anthology of feminist poetry, included some of Revati's poems. The anthology itself, planned as a political statement by feminist poets, was directed more toward polemics than poetry. The introduction to the anthology did not have anything to say about Revati.

Revati's poems are in a class by themselves; nothing like them had ever been written before in Telugu. Revati was not a poet by conscious effort—someone who presents herself as a poet to the literary world. Her language is direct, disarmingly straightforward, unpremeditated; it is self-expression in its purest sense. Her words and sentences, fresh with a nascent energy, appear on the page utterly unaware of their presence in the world of poetry. In fact, they were not poetic before Revati used them. Her passion, her sensuality, her burning desire to speak, and her discovery of the world through language, reveal a vulnerable person and an invincible poet, giving us flashes of insight into her very female world. She wrote only a small volume of poetry, but every poem in the volume is precious.

The emergence of women as feminist poets, however, has changed the literary scene. Women now give poetry readings, participate in literary seminars, and play their role as prominent leaders of literature. They write literary criticism, respond to public debates on literature, and write on social and political issues. Most important, they have changed the language of poetry in ways that are gradually being recognized. They have brought about a change in literary taste and in the use of cultural symbols. A woman's desire, the pleasure she enjoys, the pain she suffers: these are now available for literary language. Menstruation, pregnancy, and abortion are now accepted as subjects for poetry. A language that did not even have a word for rape, and a culture that invariably blamed the victim when a woman was raped, began to change to allow for public expression of sexual atrocities and physical abuse of women. Women poets protested against the depiction of women as frail and against the use of sexually abusive language against women and against the elevation of motherhood as the only respectable symbol available for women.

If women poets are to be discussed as a group—there are a good number of them writing in the last few decades—many of them will be noteworthy for the statements they make as feminists, though as poets their energies are somewhat limited and their poems mostly rhetorical. Several of them, however, stand out with a presence and an individual voice, while also participating in the general feminist protest. I was not able to include Jayaprabha, Savitri, Vimala, and Patibandla Rajani, to name some.[23]

Dalits

Identity politics empowered many castes and communities who had remained faceless under the blanket of the grand narrative of social classes. For decades, they had been lumped into one large, undifferentiated category of masses. A significant development in the late 1980s is the emergence of Dalit poetry. Dalit is a name adopted by the former untouchable castes. For centuries, Mālas and Mādigas and other such castes of former untouchables have included major oral poets among them. Such poet-singers have held the status of priests at village festivals and rituals and sung long oral epics. Master oral narrators from Māla and Mādiga castes traditionally sing narratives such as Palnāṭi Vīrula Katha, Kāṭamarāju Katha, and Jāmba Purāṇamu. Economically and socially deprived, these castes still hold a rich mastery of the oral tradition. Modern emphasis on literacy and print culture has marginalized them as illiterate, and their narratives have not stood any chance of being recognized as products of literary creativity. Reform leaders who attempted to uplift the depressed castes, such as Gandhi and Ambedkar, failed to recognize the traditional artistic talents of these castes. However, a large number of Dalit young men and women who were educated in colleges and universities since the 1940s seem to have regained the power of their poetry.

In Andhra, political battles are fought in literature before they are fought in society. The former untouchables knew that no amount of affirmative action—reservations or quotas for jobs—would help them gain cultural confidence unless they also establish a place for themselves in literature. Clearly, the way was to occupy center stage in the contemporary literary scene, as the Marxists and feminists have done previously. After the dominant culture had determined the mode and style of poetry recognized as literary, the Dalits had to master it in order to be recognized as poets. This explains why the Dalit poets adopted free verse as their major mode of expression. A few decades ago, Jashuva (1895–1971) made an opening for the untouchable castes in the literary mainstream. He gained recognition as a poet and was received into scholarly literary circles. Now, a large number of poets contend for such recognition. Dalit poets are published in mainstream journals, Dalit literary critics represent the aesthetics and ideology of their poetry, and the Dalit statement has become a part of the public discourse. While I can not possibly give an adequate survey of the range of Dalit poetry or discuss the strong voices among Dalit poets individually, I would emphasize that Dalit poets make new images by reworking the *purāṅic* myths and turning them upside down to question the authorized languages. Satish Chandar (b. 1958) is one of the more successful poets in this subversive act of creating a reworked myth, borrowing from both Sanskritic and Christian sources. In so doing, he makes his poems speak for his community. He is angry but he expresses his anger with control and dignity, with sarcasm, tinged with a sense of humor.

A significant recent development of Dalit poetry is the emergence of Dalit women poets. Their poems in recent anthologies suggest that they are distinct from the upper-caste feminist poets on the one hand, and the Dalit male poets on the other.

Muslim Poets

The recent publication of an anthology of Muslim poets jolted the literary community into recognizing Muslims as a part of Telugu life. *Jaljalā* (1998), published by the Muslim Writers Forum with poems by some twenty-five Telugu Muslim poets, claims to be the first such anthology in Telugu. For decades, Telugu writers came from the Hindus, with significant exceptions such as Umar Ali Sha (1885–1945) who wrote during the thirties, and more recent and well-known poets such as Ismail, Smile, Afsar, and Khadar Mohiuddin. An explosion of a sizable group of Telugu writers from the Muslim community has indeed expanded the literary space beyond the limits the majority communities imagined. Many poets in this anthology are new, and come from varied backgrounds.

Khadar Mohiuddin (b. 1955) brought literary attention to the Muslim identity question. His "Birthmark" debunks the complacent liberal sensibilities of modern poetic language by exposing its ideological bankruptcy and its pseudo-liberal dullness. The long poem, which starts as a personal biography, unfolds into a story of a community meandering through the crooked lanes of history. It ends by making an indelible impression of communal hypocrisy on the consciousness of the readers.

Two poets, Afsar (b. 1964) and Shajahana (b. 1974), turn inward to explore the problem of minority existence. The dialogue in both these poets is internal but the reader is given the opportunity of overhearing, and—as in all good poetry—what you overhear is what is intended. Afsar is known for his deeply nuanced language, subtle and subversive. He works his way in a quiet voice and ends just as quietly, as if he has said nothing worthwhile, but he is devastating in his undertones.

Shajahana is an unusual poet with remarkable talent. Very new to the literary field, she made a name with a small number of poems and promises to grow to be a major poet.

Poetry and the City
The following poem is often recited in conversations among conservative literary circles in response to what they regard as an explosion in the number of modern poets:

Five, six, seven,
eight, nine,
even ten per house
in every village:

poets are popping up everywhere.

As God is my witness, I swear:
once a whole country was lucky
to have one.[24]

Without sharing this cynical view of literary creativity, expressed by an anonymous poet who was perhaps guarding his position in the field of letters, we must still note that there are an enormous number of poets in Andhra today, most of them operating in or around Hyderabad. A significant feature in the literary scene of the last two decades in Hyderabad is the demise of literary-political organizations. Poets might share a common ideology or philosophy and may be generally called feminists or Dalit writers and so on, but they are essentially individuals writing as they please. Unaffiliated to any literary or political organization and yet freely adopting a liberal, progressive agenda for their poems, these poets fill the pages of literary sections of daily newspapers. Many of them have published their own books and are well-known among literary circles. Hyderabad, which has grown into the major literary and cultural center of Andhra, provides a very hospitable climate for literary meetings, seminars, and discussions. Two significant features of literary activity in Hyderabad are *pustakāviṣkaraṇa* (book-release), a celebration organized by the poet releasing his or her new book of poems, and *kavi-sanmānam*, a felicitation of one or more poets with a cash award by a patron. The events are well-attended, prominent literary people make speeches on the occasion, and the press reports them as news. In a situation where the poet has to publish his or her own book and no publishing industry publicizes poetry, cultural practices such as these provide the needed support to the poet and create a festive literary public sphere as well. Criticism leveled against this atmosphere, however, is that it does not allow for dispassionate literary evaluation by competent reviewers, but encourages self-promotion and sycophancy. The balanced and urbane critical evaluations of contemporary poets and their poetry that Chekuri Ramarao wrote in his weekly newspaper column "Cerātalu" were helpful but not influential enough to significantly change the atmosphere.

Two poets stand prominent in this public sphere, for the awards they have won from national institutions, for the attention they have received from their admirers, and for their prolific publishing record. One is C. Narayana Reddy, who has won among others, the prestigious Jñanapith Award. The second is Gunturu Seshendra Sarma, who has won an award from Sahitya Akademi, the National Academy of Letters. One common feature between them is that they write long poems that claim epic stature. Narayana Reddy's *Viśvambhara* and Seshendra Sarma's *Nā Désam Nā Prajalu ane Ādhunika Mahābhāratamu* are extensive exercises in free verse, with themes such as the birth of human civilization and the story of contemporary India. The poems are filled with noble ideas, depicting vast civilizational events on a wide canvas.

The most significant role of poetry in the city is that it continues to constitute the public sphere. An event marking the close of the century and the millennium celebrated in Hyderabad on January 2, 2000, perhaps demonstrates this feature more powerfully than any theoretical statement about it can. On that day a group of about one hundred fifty poets gathered to read their poetry all day long, from dawn to dusk, while a group of about twenty five poets demonstrated against the reading, because for them the celebration represented the dominant power structure in society.

Individual Creativity and the Public Role of Poetry

This survey, brief as it is, demonstrates that Telugu poetry has played two distinct roles during the century: one is to serve as the public sphere for social and political expression, and the other is to support individual innovation and creative excellence. Every social/political movement, aspiration, or criticism has expressed itself in literature before it succeeded as a social reality. Poetry provided the public voice, and literature was the arena of contestation. In its role of playing the public sphere, poetry has continually incorporated poets from the lower strata of society. A checklist of poets from the early decades of the century to the present will reveal that as the decades go by, more and more women and poets from the lower castes have entered the ranks. During the last decades of the century, Dalits and other lower castes have dominated the field. It would be easy to predict that an anthology of the best poems of the twenty-first century will prominently feature poets from the castes and communities now called low. While poets in their social role generally supported liberal causes and empowered the lower castes, in their other role as creative artists they retained their individual voice, irrespective of the political opinion they held. One role did not stifle the other; the involvement of poets in social and political movements did not destroy their individuality as poets, nor did the poets who wrote in their seclusion, away from the public noise, suffer a neglect for their lack of involvement. Looking back at a century of poetry, one can find a number of good poets who have emerged from literary, political, or social movements: Krishna Sastri, Viswanatha, Sri Sri, Narayana Babu, Sishtla, Jashuva, Nagnamuni, Satish Chandar, and Khadar Mohiyuddin. One can also find an equal number of poets who were not activists in any movement, but who stand out as major poets nonetheless: Kavikondala, Bangaramma, Pathabhi, Ajanta, Bairagi, Ismail, Mohana Prasad, and Revati Devi. There were long stretches of time when literary critics were swayed by the power of ideologies, or sheer personality politics. But in the end, poetry has prevailed. The lesson of the twentieth century clearly is that poets can not be judged by their beliefs, philosophies, politics, or personality traits.

Tribute, however, should be paid to the hundreds of minor poets who wrote under the influence of the romantic, modernist, Marxist, feminist, or other movements in literature and then faded into oblivion. Anthologies of Telugu poetry from each period will show a number of poets who were active and respected during their time. They formed the nexus through which or against which more lasting poetry emerged. They are the unsung heroes of battles they did not win, but these battles would not have been fought without them.

TECHNOLOGIES OF LITERARY PRODUCTION: POETRY AND PRINT

At the beginning of the twenty-first century, it is hard to imagine a time without printing presses, computers, and photocopying machines. The printing press, introduced by the European Christian missionaries in the later decades of the eighteenth century, took a firm hold on the literati. It is interesting to note that oral versifiers embraced print and made sure that every poem they composed also appeared in print. Poetry appeared in print everywhere including newspapers. The daily *Āndhra Patrika* and the monthly journal *Bhārati*, both founded by Kasinathuni Nageswara Rao, devoted great attention to poetry. The printed book created a new genre of criticism in the form of book reviews, which lead to controversies and debates on literature.

Print, however, did not homogenize the literary community, nor did it erase the oral traditions. If anything, it strengthened the existing divisions between literary communities and created new ones when a new kind of poetry was written. While Vavilla Ramasvami Sastrulu's publishing house in Madras published classical works and books by contemporary writers who wrote in the traditional style, the Bhāvakavitvam poets had their own journals, as did the Marxists and other groups that came later.

Once poetry appeared on the printed page, the printed page determined the shape of the poem. The page is not a silent carrier of the recorded poem, it is an active participant in making the poem. Until the late nineteenth century, poetry was recited by trained performers. Poets themselves learned the skills of recitation. The performers knew by previous training where to break the line and how to make stress patterns—irrespective of the way in which the verse appeared on the written page. Before the printing press, no one read a book they were not already trained to read. Reading meant reading aloud; people always read aloud, even when they were reading for themselves. For the first time in the history of Telugu poetry, people who were not previously trained to read a poem entered the reading public. They were also reading new poems—reading for the first time, what they had not already read or heard before. The age-old classification of poetry into two categories—*dṛsya*, that which is made visible, like plays, and *śravya,* that which is made audible, like a text read by a performer to his audience—has become irrelevant. Now there is poetry read by and to oneself from a printed page—poetry that needs to be seen in print while reading.

The printed page adapted to this new readership, giving them all the help they needed to read comfortably—metrical line breaks, spaces, punctuation marks, and so on. The printed book adjusted to the new needs, announcing the title of the book and name of the author on the cover rather than at the end of the text in a colophon, as was the style in manuscripts.

Bhāvakavitvam went a step further and printed the stanza—which was as metrical as any conventional verse—with line breaks at the end of performative units, rather than at the end of the metrical lines. This was revolutionary indeed in that the poem looked very different from the conventional poem, with lines of uneven lengths flowing on the page, or justified to the left. The modern poem had arrived.

If the older poets used printing as a functional tool to produce multiple copies of their manuscripts, the Bhāvakavitvam poets took to printing with an aesthetic joy. Their books were beautifully produced, with tastefully designed cover pages; every poem was elegantly printed with adequate space surrounding it. Special imported featherweight paper was used, and books were produced with a loving attention to detail. A young poet from the royal family of Pithapuram printed his

poems with only one line per page. Sri Sri made a sensational state-
ment saying that he would want to print his *Mahāprasthānam* poems
in full-length-mirror size. This was an important semiotic change.
The shape in which the poem appeared on the page was now a part
of the poem.[25]

When modern poets took to free verse, the poem depended more
than ever on the way it appeared on the printed page, with line breaks
chosen by the poet. For many, the change also made poetry indistin-
guishable from prose, and they objected that it cheapened poetry.
Poetry without meter did not sound like poetry. Free verse came to
Telugu along with a fierce controversy about whether meter is re-
quired for poetry, whether poets who write free verse really qualify to
be called poets, and so on. The arguments were as fierce as they were
endless. Every possible position from one extreme (there can be no
poetry without meter) to the other (meter is an absolute obstacle to
poetry) were upheld. Kundurti Anjaneyulu started an organization
called the Free Verse Front and a magazine in which he would publish
nothing but free verse. Some fifty years after the acceptance of free verse
by modern poets, the argument about meter is not yet quite dead. Poets
who write for large audiences invariably use some kind of meter, con-
ventional or invented, syllabic or quantitative. Poets and critics still argue
whether free verse is good for poetry, and whether it is getting too free
for its own good. However, two variables—the printing press and the
separation of the individual from the group—have had a powerful influ-
ence on the shape of the poem and the appearance of the book.

With all the love for printing, modern poetry has not attracted
publishers. Poets print their own books and sell them with the help of
friends. This is both helpful and disastrous. Free access to publishing is
good because it eliminates interference by any outside agency between
the poet and the reader, but it also leaves the poet with no editorial
advice. Except in the case of the Bhāvakavitvam poets, for whom
Swami Sivasankara Sastri (1892–1977) took the responsibility of edit-
ing, modern poetry is published with no editorial help. Everything
written comes into print if the author is determined enough.

TELUGU LITERATURE AND INDIA'S
OTHER LITERATURES

The ideological premise on which the Sahitya Akademi was established by the government of India in 1954 is summarized by the grand statement made by Dr. S. Radhakrishnan that "Indian literature is one though written in several languages." That was a nationalist sentiment indeed. But the fact is that there is little communication in the twentieth century among the many languages of India.

In premodern India, educated people often knew more than one regional language and its literature. In addition, scholars knew transregional languages such as Sanskrit, Persian, or Urdu. The boundaries between languages were much more porous than they have become since the nationalist language movements began in the early twentieth century. However, with a few exceptions, nearly all Telugu poets who wrote in the twentieth century were language chauvinists who loved Telugu so much that they showed no interest in learning the other languages of India. They wanted little interaction with other literatures except English. Average educated readers, as well as poets, knew more about English, French, German, Russian, or Italian literatures, via their English translations, than those of neighboring Oriya, Bengali, Hindi, Marathi, Tamil, or Malayalam.

An even more significant development in the identity of language boundaries resulted from the spread of colonial linguistic theories that separated India's languages into Aryan and Dravidian.[26] A fateful error of classifying people and languages together resulted in the racial classification of India's people into Dravidians and Aryans. All those who spoke Dravidian languages were considered Dravidians and those who spoke Aryan languages were considered Aryans. In this classification Sanskrit was an Aryan language that subjugated Dravidian Tamil when the Aryans invaded the South. This new anthropology elevated Tamil to the level of a classical language rivaling Sanskrit, which in turn fueled a strong anti-Brahmin cultural movement in Tamilnadu. Telugu, which was until recently the language patronized by the Nāyaka and Maratha kings in the southern kingdoms of Thanjavur and Madurai, and which therefore enjoyed a transregional popularity, was now re-duced to the language of a single region, and a Dravidian one at that. The Telugu literary establishment did not accept Tamil as its classical language nor did they accept Telugu as a Dravidian language. A new form of Telugu nationalism began to emerge in response to the new dominance of Tamil.

Language boundaries hardened so severely that even when major Telugu poets lived in Madras, which was the capital and urban center of the composite state comprising Tamil- as well as Telugu-speaking people, they showed no interest in the Tamil literary scene around them; when they moved to Hyderabad, the former capital of the Nizam and now the capital of the new Andhra state, they entertained little interac-tion with the rich Urdu literary culture in the city. Literature from other Indian languages was rarely translated into Telugu, whereas translations from English and other European languages through English were abun-dantly available. Tolstoy, Chekhov, and Gorky were household names among the middle class. Sri Sri was influenced by Louis Aragon, Paulo Elaurd, Mayakovski, Edgar Allan Poe, Swinburne, and a host of other Russian, French, American, and English poets whom he read in English translation. But he knew nothing about Tamil Sangam literature, the poetry of the Āḷvārs, or of Kampan, Bharati, or any contemporary writer from the neighborhood in Madras where he lived most of his adult life.

With the minor exception of Bengali poetry, which was read in Bengali by several Bhāvakavitvam poets educated at Santiniketan, and fiction by Saratchandra Chatterjee, which was translated from the original Bengali, all literature from other Indian languages was read in English translation. If Tagore was well-known among the educated people in Andhra during the Bhāvakavitvam period, it was because his books were extensively available in English translation. Most transla-tions from other Indian languages into Telugu are done via an English translation, with no knowledge of the original language in which the book is written. If a literary work is not available in English, its chances of being known in Andhra are very slim. If major movements in literature such as romanticism, modernism, surrealism, Marxism, feminism, and Dalitism have occurred as pan-Indian phenomena, it is more because of the influence of English or a common socio-political context—not so much from a direct interaction between the literatures of the different regions of India. Modern Telugu literature is language-locked, almost completely unaware of its neighbors' literatures, in very much the same way as the other regional literatures of India are. In the area of languages, the nationalist project has succeeded a little too well.

NOTES

1. For a view of the Nāyaka period literary scene, see Velcheru Narayana Rao, David Shulman, and Sanjay Subrahmanyam, *Symbols of Substance: Court and State in Nāyaka Period Tamil Nadu* (Delhi: Oxford University Press, 1992), especially chapter 4. Also see, A. K. Ramanujan, Velcheru Narayana Rao, and David Shulman, *When God Is a Customer: Telugu Courtesan Songs by Ksetrayya and Others* (Berkeley: University of California Press, 1994).

2. Literary theorists classified the literary genres of this period into four groups: *āśu* (oral), *madhura* (lyrical), *citra* (picturesque), and *vistara* (narrative).

3. For an introduction to the *cāṭu* world in Telugu, Tamil, and Sanskrit, see Velcheru Narayana Rao and David Shulman, *A Poem at the Right Moment: Remembered Verses from Premodern South India* (Berkeley: University of California Press, 1998), especially the After-Essay.

4. Recent historical scholarship contends that much of the military, fiscal, commercial, and trade superiority of the European companies was not a given, but was equally matched by the various eighteenth century Indian polities. See C. Bayly, *Rulers, Townsmen, Bazaars: North Indian Society in the Age of British Expansion* (Cambridge: Cambridge University Press, 1983); C. A. Bayly and Sanjay Subrahmanyam, "Portfolio Capitalists and the Political Economy of Early Modern India," *Indian Economic and Social History Review* 25 (1988); and Rajanarayan Chandavarkar, *The Origins of Industrial Capitalism in India: Business Strategies and the Working Class in Bombay, 1900–1940* (Cambridge: Cambridge University Press, 1994), 21–71. Until recently, capitalism was thought to have been the exclusive domain of European history introduced to the rest of the world through colonial enterprise. This point is particularly pronounced in the argument of World Systems Theorists such as Immanuel Wallerstein. David Washbrook ("South Asia, the World System, and World Capitalism," *Journal of Asian Studies* 49, no. 3 [August 1990]: 479–508) and others (cf. Sugata Bose, ed., *South Asia and World Capitalism* [Delhi: Oxford University Press, 1990]) aptly question the assumptions of Wallerstein's model. Max Weber and many of his intellectual followers found caste in India to be a hindrance to the development of complex finance, commerce, and trade necessary for the development of capitalistic potentialities. See David Rudner,

Caste and Capitalism in Colonial India: The Nattukottai Chettiars (Berkeley: University of California Press, 1994) for an excellent treatment of the role of caste organization in the complex world of capitalist finance during the nineteenth century. Finally, for a recent study of the role of science in the making of modern India, see Gyan Prakash, *Another Reason: Science and the Imagination of Modern India* (Princeton: Princeton University Press, 1999).

5. Guari Viswanathan, *Masks of Conquest: Literary Study and British Rule in India* (New York: Columbia University Press, 1989).

6. The colonial government enacted laws against books with erotic descriptions, and printers were forced either to publish them in limited editions, under an agreement to sell to scholars only, or to remove verses considered obscene. Such legislation against immorality in literature was common in other language areas too. For a case study of Bengal, see Tapti Roy, "Disciplining the Printed Text: Colonial and Nationalist Surveillance of Bengali Literature," in *Texts of Power: Emerging Disciplines of Colonial Bengal,* ed. Partha Chatterjee (Minneapolis: University of Minnesota Press, 1995), 30–62.

7. The story of Bilhaṇa is interesting for its long textual-critical life from the eleventh century onward and its geographical spread across all of India. Barbara S. Miller's translation (*Phantasies of a Love-Thief: The Caura Pancasika Attributed to Bilhaṇa* [New York: Columbia University Press, 1971]) includes a critical edition that explores the spatial variation of the themes and highlights the differences in the traditions of the North and South. Citrakavi Singaracarya, a late-eighteenth-century Telugu poet, adopts the Sanskrit story for his *Bilhaṇiyamu,* which has been printed many times since 1873. In 1961, Vavilla Ramasvami Sastrulu & Sons, Madras, published it as a "scholars' edition, for private circulation only," and M. Seshacalam & Company, Machilipatnam, published a critical edition, edited by Bommakanti Venkata Singaracharya and Balantrapu Nalinikantarao, in 1971.

8. Reddy was a powerful man. He had a degree from England, which in itself was regarded with great respect and assured his promotion to important political and academic roles in Andhra. In his politics he was conservative and supported the British colonial government, which rewarded him with a knighthood. He rose to occupy the position of the first Vice Chancellor of the newly established Andhra University in Visakhapatnam. *NavaYāmini* became required reading for every cultured Telugu person.

Earlier, in his play *Bilhaṇiyamu,* which he left incomplete, Gurajada Apparao depicts Bilhaṇa as a more intensely sensuous person. We learn from the outline of the play found in the author's papers that Bilhaṇa finds the princess irresistible but he leaves town. The reasons for his action are not entirely clear from the outline Apparao wrote, but it appears that fear of transgression is not one of them. I am writing a separate study of Apprarao's *Bilhaṇiyamu.*

9. Cattamanchi Ramalinga Reddy, *Kavitva-tattva-vicāramu* (1914; reprint, Waltair: Andhra University Press, 1980).

10. For a discussion of Tirupati Sastri's and Venkata Sastri's poems in oral circulation, see Velcheru Narayana Rao and David Shulman, *A Poem at the Right Moment: Remembered Verses from Premodern South India* (Berkeley: University of California Press, 1998).

11. Rao and Shulman, *A Poem at the Right Moment*, 47.

12. Rayaprolu Subbarao was trained at Santiniketan, Rabindranath Tagore's school for the arts. The influence of Tagore's ideas on Rayaprolu and others of his generation can not be underestimated. As a Nobel Prize winner, and as the first Asian to do so, Tagore had a supreme position among writers of his generation.

13. One such legend relates to a period when Krishna Sastri agreed late in his life to work as a producer at All India Radio. He was sitting on the lawn of the radio station, chatting with another poet, Katuri Venkateswara Rao, and enjoying a cigar with him, when word was brought to him that the Minister for Broadcasting, who was visiting, wanted to see him. Krishna Sastri reportedly answered, "A great poet is here to see me; I am busy and can't come now." He accepted no one as his superior. Even when he was invited to give a talk, he generally arrived hours late, but his audiences waited for him in the hundreds. Once he arrived, he captivated them with his words; and his audience listened for hours as he spoke of the beauties of poetry—the new poetry written by his friends in the Bhāvakavitvam movement

14. Krishna Sastri was an engaging conversationalist. He lived a life of comfort and style, always surrounded by friends and admirers. Since he was independently wealthy, he never had to work for a living. But if his youth was happy, his old age was tragic. In 1963 he lost his larynx to cancer and could not speak for the rest of his life. He still received visitors and wrote his part of the conversation on a small notebook with a pen specially made of fragrant sandalwood. Seeing him in that condition, one was reminded of lines from a poem he had written in his youth: "Even in my silenced voice you can hear / murmurs of sleeping mountain streams."

15. Vedula Satyanarayana Sastri, "Aradhana," in *Vaitāḷikulu* (1935; Vijayawada: Adarsa Grantha Mandali, 1966), 69.

16. Basavaraju Apparao, *Basavaraju Apparavu Gitalu* (Rajahmundry: Kalahasti Tammaravu & Sons, 1955), 64.

17. These lines are from "Konte Konalu," *Sri Sri Sahityam*, vol. 2, part 1, ed. K. V. Ramana Reddy (Madras: 1970), 140.

18. When it was sent to *Bhārati,* the leading literary magazine of the time, it was returned with thanks, but was published in *Jvāla,* a magazine of the young poets. Sri Sri himself gave this information in his autobiography (*Anantam*

[Visakhapatnam: Virasam Pracurana 1986], 181), but did not identify the name of the journal that rejected the poem.

19. The government did not take too kindly to this literary development, which was provoking political upheaval. It used the state machinery to repress the movement. Poets and singers were jailed, and their publications were banned. Subbarao Panigrahi was killed by the police in what they claimed was an act of self-defense. The civil liberties organizations, however, claimed it was a staged encounter.

20. Viswanatha Satyanarayana, *Venaraju* (1935; Vijayawada: V.S.N. & Co, 1970), 29.

21. Rao and Shulman, *A Poem at the Right Moment*, 51.

22. Ibid., 50.

23. For poems by Jayaprabha, Savitri, and Vimala, see Arlene R. K. Zide, *In Their Own Voice: Anthology of Contemporary Indian Women Poets* (New Delhi: Penguin Books, 1993).

24. Rao and Shulman, *A Poem at the Right Moment*, 79.

25. Outside the world of poetry, the printing press brought prose into popular use. Gidugu Ramamurti (1863–1940) argued in favor of adopting a prose style based on the language used in educated speech, and Gurajada Apparao employed spoken Telugu for his fiction and plays. In writing poetry, however, everyone was stuck using old Telugu words. This was because syllabic meters did not allow for laxity in the canonical shape of the word. It was not just a matter of choice for the poet; it was the limitation of the meters. Poets, however modern they were in their ideas and images, still followed conventional meters. A tradition that had held sway for almost nine hundred years was not easy to abandon.

26. For an excellent study of this question see Thomas R. Trautmann, *Aryans and British India* (Berkeley: University of California Press, 1997).

INDEX